MARESFIELD LIBRARY

DREAM ANALYSIS

A PRACTICAL HANDBOOK FOR PSYCHO-ANALYSTS

BY

ELLA FREEMAN SHARPE

WITH AN INTRODUCTION BY

M. MASUD R. KHAN

MARESFIELD LIBRARY
LONDON

First Published 1937
Second Impression 1949
Third Impression 1951
Fourth Impression 1959
Fifth Impression 1961
New Edition first Published 1978
Reprinted 1988 with the
permission of Hogarth Press Ltd by
H. Karnac (Books) Ltd
58 Gloucester Road
London SW7 4QY

Printed & bound in Great Britain by
print in black, Midsomer Norton, Bath

ISBN 0946439 45 1

CONTENTS

WITH MY GRATITUDE
TO
THOSE WHO TOLD ME THESE DREAMS

INTRODUCTION

by M. Masud R. Khan

*'She had green translucent eyes
and an enveloping gaze'.*
                    Sylvia Payne

ELLA SHARPE was of Mohammed's persuasion: if the mountain would not come to her, she would go to the mountain. And so she travelled to Vienna, in her fifties, and in the twenties of this century, to find psychoanalysis; and she was not a young acolyte, but someone firmly established in her own discipline of literature and teaching. With Hanns Sachs, another non-medical analyst of great distinction in Freud's *entourage intellectuelle*, she found her metier.

Ella Sharpe was the first person to recognise that the dream-work and the grammatical structure of language are of one and the same order. As Dr. Jacques Lacan was to say some twenty years later, "l'inconscient est structuré comme un langage". Ella Sharpe furthermore recognised the dream as metaphor, the metaphor which is a *collage* of mind and body. As Groddeck knew only too well! Ella Sharpe was one of perhaps three persons who had the confidence to know that she was a humble heir apparent, absolutely convinced of her

9

virtue but, at the same time, anonymous. It is a great privilege for me to have been asked to write this Introduction. I was Ella Sharpe's last analysand. I salute her, and I hope that all those who read her work will do the same.

Ella Sharpe knew in an uncanny way that all language is born of the body, but she went further and also realised that what the mind creates as language can betray the body, just as the body can distort what is the insinuation and cognitive virtue of the mind.

Man is the only animal who dreams and has both the need and the capacity to make and tell his dreams. Hence the necessity of *language*, that unique invention of man, which has created all human cultures and civilisations. For centuries upon centuries men dreamt and made their dreams fatedness or conquest. Then towards the end of the nineteenth century a man dreamt, and interpreted his own dream: FREUD. He had the resourcefulness to say it was *his* dream and seek its meaning the hard way. To escape into mystical hermeneutics would have been too easy.

Language is man's prerogative, and it was Freud who was left to speak that if man is Darwin's animal, he is also someone more: he *dreams*! And Freud spelt out the grammar of how man dreams.

I know of few books that comprehend Freud's message with such clarity and acumen as Ella Sharpe's. She shows us, as Dr. Lacan was to do decades later, that the grammar of language and the dream-work are consentient, to borrow a phrase from Coleridge.

September 1977

A NOTE TO READERS

THIS book gives permanent form to the lectures on "Dreams" given to the students in training under the auspices of the Institute of Psycho-Analysis, London, in the years 1934 and 1936. It is therefore addressed specifically to psycho-analysts engaged in practical therapy. The theory of dream psychology is not re-stated in this book, some knowledge of it being assumed. In addition to Freud's work on *The Interpretation of Dreams*, students attending the lectures referred to above were recommended to the chapters on "Freud's Theory of Dreams" and "The Theory of Symbolism" in Ernest Jones's work *Papers on Psycho-Analysis* as the most compact summary of Freud's work on dreams.

In this book the theory of dream psychology is illustrated in detail by the examination of specific dream material gathered during the course of my own analytic work with neurotic and normal persons. The elucidation of dream mechanisms, various methods of evaluating dreams and the technique of dream interpretation fall within the scope of this book.

I take this opportunity of thanking my colleagues on the Training Committee for the unfailing encouragement and help I received from them while preparing this book for publication. The president of the Training Committee during the years 1934 and 1936 was Dr. Ernest Jones, the secretary Dr. Edward Glover, and other members were Dr. Sylvia Payne, Dr. John Rickman, Mrs. Klein and myself.

To Dr. Ernest Jones I am especially indebted for his invaluable criticism, both scientific and literary, of the original MS.

9 Kent Terrace,
   Regent's Park,
      London, N.W.1.

CHAPTER I

THE DREAM AS A TYPICAL AND INDIVIDUAL PSYCHICAL PRODUCT

1. The dream as a typical psychical functioning.
2. The dream as an individual psychical product. Intuition, experienced knowledge and expression are aspects of one fact.
3. The unknown is implicit in the known. The revelation of the unknown from the known underlies all valid dream interpretation.
4. The principles of poetic diction and their derivation from dream mechanisms with illustrative dream material.
5. The basis of language is implied metaphor. The importance of this fact as an aid to the interpretation of dreams. Illustrative material.

DREAMING is a universal psychical functioning, common alike to primitive and cultured peoples. It is a psychical activity inseparable from life itself, for the only dreamless state is death. Dreams may not be remembered in waking consciousness, but subterranean psychical activity is, while life lasts, as unceasing as physiological processes of which also we are not aware in deep sleep. The dream, then, can be considered typical of the human mind. Freud called the unconscious laws governing all dream productions, condensation, displacement, symbolization and secondary elaboration. In addition to these general unconscious laws responsible for the formation of dreams he postulated the unconscious mind as the source of unceasing psychical activity which during sleep represented its wishes in dreams.

13

The dream reveals within itself those unconscious mental mechanisms evolved during the course of development for the purpose of controlling and shaping the primitive instinctual self towards that norm of behaviour demanded by the contemporary civilization.

A working knowledge of the dream as a typical functioning of the psyche—that is, a knowledge of the dream mechanisms and of the theory of unconscious symbolism—is therefore indispensable for dream interpretation. This knowledge may be gained intellectually from the recommended books, but emotional conviction is the result only of personal analytic experience.

I will turn next to the individual aspect of dreams. In addition to the knowledge I have indicated as necessary in the attempt to interpret dreams, one needs to possess also specific knowledge of the person whose dreams are subjected to interpretation. Typical as are the dream mechanisms, the unconscious symbolism and the indestructible primitive wishes, the dream is yet the key to an individual psychical orientation inseparable from that individual's reaction to a specific environment within a specific period of time. (Dreams indicate the cultural environment of the individual.[1]) The dream-life holds within itself not only the evidence of our instinctual drives and the mechanisms by which those drives are harnessed or neutralized, but also the actual experiences through which we have passed.

Dreams should be considered as an individual psychical product from a storehouse of specific

[1] J. Steward Lincoln. *The Dream in Primitive Cultures.* 1935.

experience, which indeed the dreamer may in consciousness neither remember nor know that he knows. The material composing the latest content of a dream is derived from *experience* of some kind. All intuitive knowledge is experienced knowledge. Just as a child's play is evidence of both wish and experience, so the dream however alien to consciousness is the expression of personal experience. I am using the term " experience " here to include not only actual past occurrences but the emotional states and bodily sensations painful and pleasurable accompanying such occurrences.

In this respect one may make a comparison between dreams and works of art. To an artist forgotten experience seems accessible in some way so that it can be utilized although there may be no conscious awareness that past knowledge is part of his creative imagination. One would surmise, for example, that the repetition of a particular type of lighting in Rembrandt's pictures is determined by a predilection rooted in forgotten experience. Turner repeatedly introduces a similar bridge into landscapes which were inspired by countries widely separated geographically. The following analytic material illuminates the argument.

A patient brought a sketch of his own to show me. He said it was not entirely a reproduction of a landscape he had seen. The woodland depicted was definitely a reproduction of a scene he had enjoyed during his holiday, " but," he said, " there was nothing of that sort in the glen," and he pointed to a large solitary rock in the middle of it. " That," he said, " was an invention of my own. I saw nothing like that in the actual scenery before me."

Twelve months after this analytic episode we were working upon a series of dreams, the details of which are not necessary for my present purpose. In each dream of the series occurred two female figures. The investigation of the significance of the women in the dream finally resulted in his saying, " Of course the first little girl I remember meeting was when I was four years of age. She was my own age. I remember nothing about her except my dislike of her." Then he added, " I have not thought for years of the place where I spent that holiday. I remember now one of the strangest things about it. There was a huge isolated rock in the district, and of course any visitor to this town goes to see it."

The forgotten experience at the age of four was therefore first of all manifested as an impulse to put a rock in a glen in his picture. The artist " invented " something. He did not know in consciousness that he had seen that rock. Further analysis revealed that the rock itself was remembered whereas the emotional experience which made him dislike the little girl was forgotten.

The picture on the dream-canvas contains in the same way elements of the forgotten past. The dream as a means of evocation of association that will bring to consciousness forgotten experience and its allied emotion is one of its main values in psycho-analytic technique.

A successful analysis results in the enlargement of the ego-boundaries. This involves a complicated psychical readjustment achieved through the dynamics of the transference. We can think of this extension of the ego-boundaries as the increased

power of the ego to tolerate and deal with instinctual impulses in a rational and effective way within
a socialized community, this being achieved pro-
portionally to the modification of the unconscious
super-ego.

In this process the dream is a help not only in the
recovery of specific past emotional situations or
phantasied ones but also in the correlation between
these and the affects felt towards the analyst. The
ego therefore becomes strengthened by the recovery
of a past it is no longer necessary to deny or ignore
both on its own account or on account of others.
The past becomes assimilated and mastered through
emotional re-living and understanding, and the
personality becomes enriched through a transvaluation of past experiences. Not only is the
psychical ego extended but bodily powers themselves are enhanced, recovered or developed. Of
these the attainment of sexual potency is to be
correlated with the possibility of the fullest psychical
efficiency in a reality world.

In cases of impaired body-ego functioning such
as psychical deafness and a considerable loss of
vision I have found dreams very useful as a means
of indicating specific situations in which denial of
hearing and seeing became necessary through
psychical fears. Such dreams are invaluable as an
aid to the recognition of the repetition of the past
in the transference setting.

The dream manifests the timelessness of the unconscious mind. It regards neither the temporal
nor spatial factors that characterize reality. The
reservoir of Id energy supplying the force we
utilize in all our activities has no cognizance of

time and space. Our essential life knows no mortality. Hence the vitality in extreme age of those whose psychical life is happily adjusted. On the other hand when it is not so adjusted the psychical fixations at early stages of development themselves become timeless and ubiquitous. The dream again is a useful means in analytic treatment of revealing both the stage of development and type of fixation to which the psyche is tethered.

I return now from these considerations of dreams as a means of understanding the specific personal vicissitudes in experience to the subject of the scope of this book.

I shall not attempt the complete interpretation of any dream, not even when I devote a whole chapter to a single dream. I shall confine myself strictly to the actual material given to me by the patient in the course of one session. I wish to give samples of material from the ordinary course of analytic work. Such sessions will be full of significances and revelations that any competent worker can hope to find, and also what is quite as important to realize they will be full of obscurities that are inevitable in an unfolding psychical pattern.

In analysis one would say that the assimilation of knowledge of the unconscious mind through the ego is an essential part of the psychical process. The principle involved in valid explanation is the revelation of the unknown, implicit in the known, in terms of the individual. This principle underlies all true dream interpretation.

Proceeding upon the principle of revealing the unknown implicit in the known, I propose to approach the subject of dream mechanisms through the avenue of the accepted characteristics of poetic diction.

The laws of poetic diction were not in the first place originated by the critics of æsthetics to the purposed end of evoking good verse from the poet. They were formulated and codified from an intellectual critical survey of poetry itself. These laws are inherent and intrinsic in the best verse and so may be regarded as being the product of the closest co-operation between preconscious and unconscious activity. " I sing but as the linnets may and pipe because I must." The laws of poetic diction, evolved by the critics from great poetry and the laws of dream formation as discovered by Freud, spring from the same unconscious sources and have many mechanisms in common.

[1]Poetic diction should be " simple, sensuous, and passionate " (Milton), for the poet's task is to communicate *experience*. The basic means of communication for him is by sound and allied with that is the power of evoking imagery. To this end poetic diction prefers picturesque imagery to the enumeration of facts, it avoids the generic term and selects the particular. It is averse to lengthiness and dispenses with conjunction and relative pronoun where possible. It substitutes epithets for phrases. By means such as these a poem appeals to ear and eye and becomes an animated canvas.

The simplest of all poetic devices is the figure of speech called simile. (Note in passing the phrase " figure of speech." I shall refer to implied metaphor in another part of this lecture.) By simile is meant the equation of two dissimilar things by means of a

[1] Bradley and Seeley. *English Lessons for English People.*

common attribute, the similarity being expressed by means of the words " as " and " like."

> Blue were her eyes as the fairy flax,
> Her cheeks like the dawn of day,
> And her bosom white as the hawthorn buds
> That ope in the month of May.

Similarity of relationship may be expressed by simile, as for example, " The plough turns up the land as the ship furrows the sea." A compressed simile is called a metaphor, the words " like " and " as " being omitted. A transference of relationship can be made between one set of objects to another, for example, " The ship ploughs the sea."

Omitting for the time being the important problem of true symbolism in the theory of dream formation, and thinking only in terms of simile and metaphor as known in poetic diction, I will give you a dream which illustrates very simply these figures of speech. They are to be found both in the dream and in the dreamer's elaboration of the dream content.

" *I was at a concert and yet the concert was like a feeding. I could somehow see the music pass before my eyes like pictures. The music pictures passed like ships in the night. There were two sorts of pictures, white mountains with softly rounded tops, and others following them were tall and pointed.*"

We have in this dream first of all the simile, " The concert was like a feeding." " The music passed like pictures." We have metaphor in the context of " Ships that pass in the night and speak each other in passing." The ships imply human beings (they speak) and the dreamer knows this although it is not explicitly stated.

Only in one particular do we need to call upon our knowledge of unconscious symbolism to help us interpret the dream, namely, in the matter of the pictures of softly rounded and pointed mountains. The rest is given in simile and metaphor.

I would like to point out other simple things about this dream, which because simple are none the less profound and because obvious the more likely to be overlooked. In the first place this dream bears witness to actual experiences, namely, the actual seeing of rounded and pointed mountains in pictures or in landscape and a correlation made by the observer on first seeing such pictures with the sight in reality of breasts and penis. Secondly, it bears witness to the child's wish to be fed at night-time and of the child's phantasy on seeing the father's penis that it too was a feeding place. " Ships that pass in the night and speak each other in passing." So we read the dream wish. The great parents like ships in the night are friendly to each other. The child is secure in the plenitude of supply from both. The poignancy of the dream lay in the fact that in reality the patient was suffering from the loss by death of a beloved one. This loss had stirred memories to the depths of infantile frustration and desire. Notice too the importance of music as an unconscious selection of a possible sublimation of frustrated oral desire. Expressed by a poet it runs:

If music be the food of love play on.

21

I will pass next to a device employed by poetic diction known as personal metaphor in which a transference of personal relations is made to an impersonal object. Poetic diction uses such phrases as, " a prattling brook," " the sighing oak," " a frowning mountain," phrases which transfer human activities on to the non-human. This device in poetic diction is a derivative of unconscious mechanisms in dreams for a flowing stream in a dream will by association suggest both a stream of urine and a flow of talk. Trees in dreams are objects on to which personal attributes are often transferred. The particular tree chosen by the dreamer will be specific to the purpose of the dream. " Bay trees " and " beech trees " I have found selected because the person whom the tree signified was once seen on a seashore. " Yew " trees I have found indicated the transference on to the analyst of an unconscious imago (you). A " pine " tree I have found indicating an unconscious longing for the person the tree represented, a " birch tree " the representation of a punishing parental image, while a " Scotch fir " has not only indicated the nationality of the parental figure, but the repressed experience of observing on the parental body hair which has been unconsciously likened to fur.

The poetic device of metonymy means literally " a change of name." In this device a name that has a usual or even an accidental connection with a thing is used to indicate the thing itself. We speak, for example, of " the bar," " the bench," when we mean the profession of the law. Other examples among many are the " Woolsack," " the Chair," " the Crown." Metonymy serves as an economy in words and at the same time calls up a pictorial image. In dream mechanisms it aids the work of the censorship since the latent content will concern the thing itself and the manifest content the thing connected with it. In the dream, "*I take a piece of silk from a cupboard and destroy it*," I found that silk as silk *per se* stimulated no important associations, while the phrase "take silk" brought real emotional understanding, because "take silk" is the device of metonymy and means "to be called to the bar," i.e. to become a barrister. The first more superficial meaning of the dream was the hatred the dreamer had of his profession and on further analysis the dream revealed repressed hostile feelings towards the man's father who was himself a lawyer. Here is another example of the same device. The dreamer seemed to think that in her dream *a baby had just been delivered. The top part of its face was slatey-coloured.* Considerable anxiety was felt in the dream because of this last feature. Experiences connected with gynæcological work were the immediate associations, but these evoked no affect. This was released after the simple realization that "slatey-coloured" in actual experience will first of all be associated with slates (i.e. metonymy). "*Slates*" recalled a memory of the burial of a doll and a slate erected as a tombstone. An outburst of affect accompanied the recollection, and the unrecognized wish in the dream became clearer when in addition to the foregoing the patient recalled the tombstones of two little children of her mother's who had died before the patient was born, and phantasies of her own about her mother's womb.

Another common example of this figure of speech is in the use of the word " table." We speak of a person keeping a " good table," meaning thereby food and not the actual table. Leaving aside at the moment the question of symbolism, a knowledge of ordinary speech usage will lead us aright in the deduction that a dream of a table will at least indicate a reference to food. The first table supplying food is the mother's body. A *mackintosh* in a dream should direct our attention to its association with water. A visual image in a dream of water which the patient describes as a " sheet of water " should lead us directly to water associated with *sheets*. A " *chair* " should direct us to the finding of the associated person *sitting* in it, a dress to the *body* of the person wearing the dress. Here is a pleasing and simple example of this same device in a dream. " *You were sitting in a deck-chair wearing a sailor hat.*" Let us forget unconscious symbolism for the moment and pursue only this device of metonymy. "A sailor hat," said my patient with the ingenuousness of the direct child, "will be a hat belonging to a sailor, and as you were sitting in a deck-chair it means you represent a sailor." "What kind of a sailor ? " I queried. " Well, I once told my mother you looked like a pirate." " Which pirate ? " I asked. " Oh, Captain Hook, I'm sure." We were then launched on a wealth of phantasy concerning the nefarious practices of pirates in comparison with which the bald interpretation of a sailor hat as unconsciously meaning a phallus would have been barren indeed. Two days after this dream the patient was deep in reverie concerning the problem of the protective efficiency of her nails and suddenly she had the horrid idea of long claws that could catch into things. " Captain Hook " was still being an active stimulus in her phantasy life !

I will make an interpolation here regarding technique in dream interpretation. You will have noticed the questions I put to the patient: " What kind of sailor ? " " Which pirate ? " The reason for such questions regarding details in dreams is to be found in the principle that is explicit in the rules of poetic diction and implicit in the unconscious dream mechanisms. Poetic diction prefers the particular to the generic term and in dream inter-pretation we gain understanding by the pursuit of a particular reference from any general term. Hence the analyst will not be content with the association of " a sailor " nor even of " a pirate," which was this patient's next association, but should follow up with the specific question " Which pirate ? " We must remember the latent material is specific to the individual, and that even in the matter of symbolism, the symbols themselves are indicative of a specific environment.

Synecdoche is a figure of speech in which a part does duty for the whole. We speak of a fleet of so many " sails," of a factory accommodating so many " hands." " Oh, is it fish, or weed, or maiden's hair ? " the poet says, meaning that if it is hair he sees a *maiden* is drowned. In the music dream I quoted the " parts " signified the " whole." Breasts and penis were represented symbolically yet the total body was indicated in the image " Ships that pass in the night." The devices of metonymy and synecdoche are both illustrated in the case of the shoe fetish. On to the shoe is transferred the significance of the foot, but during the course of analysis one finds that the foot as a part of the body can not only take over the attributes of other parts of the body, but can represent the whole body as well. The following are further examples taken from dream material. "A scarlet pimpernel" evoked latent thoughts about the nipple. "A tangle of thorn bushes" and "a box hedge" represented pubic hair, and pubic hair itself evoked latent phantasies concerning the concealed female genital. "Box hedge" is particularly apt, box itself being a common vulval symbol.

Onomatopœia is the poetic device used when the sounds of words employed echo the sense. Our language is rich in such words and the dream will often employ them since the psyche has at its disposal early personal experiences when sound was fused with meaning. We repeat in the individual acquisition of language something of the history of the development of language itself. Single letters can carry over in a dream the most primitive sounds allied with infantile experiences. I am indebted to a patient for the following interesting corroborative dream material. *In the dream she was narrating was a combination of letters " K. OH." which had a chemical reference.* In telling me the dream she said " S.O.S." instead of " K.OH." and then she corrected herself thus: " I said S.O.S. inadvertently, I meant to say K.OH." The formula K.OH. in the dream finally yielded by associations the significance of " Ka.Ka." the child's word for fæces. It was the inadvertently expressed " S.O.S." which finally was of most interest, for " S.O.S." is a present-day signal for distress. " S " proved to be the hissing sound of urine inadvertently passed and the " O " the involuntary sound of distress often made by a child when such an accident happens. Etymological research has led students to conjecture that the present tense of the verb " to be," that is, " is," probably one of our most fundamental words, was in its origin the imitation of the actual sound of running water, thus meaning " life," " being." Hence in this dream, together with the inadvertent " S.O.S." we had in a purely verbal form the dramatization of a forgotten childhood anxiety situation. Our present-day signal of distress employed by ships at sea, " S.O.S.," contains then a wealth of unsuspected meaning in its brevity and usefulness in an elemental danger situation on water.

The devices in diction known as " parallel " and " antithesis " are possible in a dream by means of pictures. Antithesis for instance can be conveyed by opposition in position, as, for example, " I sat opposite to her." Parallels can be conveyed by similarity of position. " You were sitting in a chair and alongside you was sitting X." Even to understand this simple device can be of immediate usefulness in interpretation for if " You " refers to the analyst and " X " is a person unknown to the analyst then whatever is said by the patient about " X " will in some way apply to " You."

Repetition of phrases is a device in diction to secure emphasis. The method employed in the dream is the repetition of some dream element.

I will now turn to the consideration in more detail of the figure of speech called " implied metaphor." A great part of our ordinary language is implied metaphor. Things that are not tangible and visible are described by means of the relationship of those that are. Words expressing mental and moral states are based upon an analogy drawn between mind and body. A very few examples will suffice as illustration, such as " a striking thought," " a wealth of knowledge," " food for thought," " a spotless character," " a brown study," " a hot temper." The sense of hearing being less powerful than the senses of taste, touch and sight, the poorer sense borrows from the richer when epithets are required to describe sound. Hence we have implied metaphor in such descriptions of sound as " a sweet voice," " a piercing scream." Words have a history of displacement individually as well as racially from the first context in which we heard them, when they designated some definite sensible image. Words acquire a second meaning and convey abstract ideas, but they do not lose as far as the unconscious storehouse of our past is concerned the concrete significance the words possessed when we first heard and used them. The individuality of a word consists in the sum of its past and present significations. The value of a dream therefore lies not only in discovering the latent material by means of the manifest content, but the language used in the narration of dream and in the giving of associations will itself help towards elucidation. Apart from other psychical values that follow from self-expression as such, the very language used in self-expression will itself yield up significance. To take full advantage of this we need to remember that words will not only carry a secondary meaning but implicitly also a primary one. We need to be alive to their historical past, and to the fact that that historical past will often convey the historical past of the speaker. Here are two simple examples; " I dreamt of X, she is her mother's spoiled darling." The patient in saying this meant that X was pampered. She was using the secondary meaning of " spoiled." Its other meaning for any child will be marred, dirtied, ruined, just as etymologically the word means " to skin or mar." An analyst who remembers this is likely to reach the significance of the dream more quickly than one who does not. Here is another example. " *I dreamt I was speculating on the Stock Exchange.*" The patient's associations will in the first place be concerned with the theme of stocks and shares but the word " speculating " should suggest to the analyst that the fundamental *primary* activity indicated is that of looking. The " Stock Exchange " will then be worth further consideration in the same way. To repeat then, one great value of directing a patient's attention to elaborating the dream is that it gives the analyst an opportunity to interpret dreams more fully from the actual words chosen by the patient. The [1]bridges of thought are crossed and re-crossed by names and names have manifold mutations. We must remember that the dream will evoke words that connote and include many significances in contrast with scientific words which are the most exclusive. The dream that is abstractly expressed will only become serviceable to us analytically when it can be translated pictorially. We must reach the primary meaning of words underlying

[1] George Willis. *Philosophy of Speech.* 1919.

the secondary. Concrete terms owing to their origins are infinitely richer in associations than abstract ones.

I pass now from implied metaphor, by means of which knowledge we have the key for analysis of abstract phraseology, to the consideration of the concrete terms themselves. I would draw your attention first to the well-known capacity on the part of the unconscious mind in the art of punning. Should we be more correct in looking upon this both in dreams and in conversation as a glimpse of the way in which we learned words in the first instance, that is, phonetically ? Only rarely by dreams and odd memories do we get even a slight conception of this phonetic ramification, carrying with it ideas of one signification on to new words that *sound* like the ones we heard first. We have here a fruitful field for investigation. We need to remember that the sound of a word and its first significance will be implicit in another word (or phrases) of the same sound but of different meaning. Here is an example. " *I dream of Iona Cathedral.*" This is not merely an example of punning. It is a fragment of history in the child's acquisition of language. The first time the dreamer as a child heard the word " Iona " it sounded and meant to him " I own a cathedral." I am indebted to the same patient for the following memory. His father promised to bring him *The Lays of Ancient Rome* and the son thought that his father would give him a present of eggs.

I will continue with further examples which illustrate this importance of verbal expression and how our awareness of the acquisition of language phonetically is of use in helping us to realize the import of words. Let us remember too that expression and experienced knowledge are two aspects of one fact. Here is an admirable example. "*I was with dogs and about to go on an allotment but I was warned that it was dangerous. It seemed it was dangerous to tread on the ground as if it were infectious.*" I will give only a few pertinent associations. The infection suggested to the patient " foot and mouth " disease. One dog in the dream seemed to be a greyhound. Two successive toys of the patient's early childhood were " Grey Bunny " and " Long Dog." " Foot and mouth " instantly suggested a childhood game of putting her foot into her mouth. The patient then informed me she was constipated. With even this one bodily reference and the given associations I have selected, one can infer fairly quickly the experiences and phantasies of episodes in her forgotten childhood. Listen to the word " a-llot-ment " instead of thinking or picturing the acquired specialized meaning of the word as we understand it to-day. The dream can then easily be apprehended through this one word. Here is another example. "*In the dream,*" the patient remarked, "*there was a courtyard.*" I am omitting from the dream many specific details in order to illustrate my immediate subject of the importance of different significations one word will imply. Here for instance " court " will suggest at least " to woo " but the *sound* of " court " will also suggest the word " caught." The word " court-yard " suggested neither of these meanings to the patient. Needless to say the analyst did not suggest them either until the patient in the course of the analytical hour spoke as follows: " Last week-end I went to X's place in —— shire. He has a little enclosed garden place and you get to it through a special gate. I went in and shut the door. When I was ready to return I found the door locked and there was no way out but by climbing the wall and that was spiked." The unconscious phantasies of the dangers of " courting " thereupon became accessible.

I have a "*feeling of depression*" was a patient's opening remark lately. The hour's analysis was concerned with anxiety regarding the female genitals. I had no hesitation finally in saying that he was dealing with repressed emotions concerning an incident some time in childhood when he *literally* felt the " depression " of a little girl's genitals. " I feel," said another patient *in response to the stimulus of a dream about food* " *that when I think of that food I used to have, there was something fæcal about it.*" Where do you *feel* it ? " I asked. " Well, I was thinking about it, I mean," he replied. Yet even as he was speaking he was unconsciously moving his fingers over one another. The experience was *in his fingers*, the knowledge of an early experience of touching fæcal matter was stored in them. In the case of a patient who is very occupied by external real interests I have to rely on phrases such as the following to evoke phantasy and memory that is implicit but unknown in consciousness. " I must start to make that garment, but I must say I am *filled with horror* at the thought." " Filled with horror " had the ultimate significance of horrible phantasies concerning the horrible things inside the body, i.e. terrifying phantasies

32

concerning procreation. "In my dream," said another patient, "*I was pulling out tin-tacks*." After many circumlocutions she returned to the dream and ruminated on the word "tin-tack." "What other name have they?" "Screws?" "No," she did not mean tin-tacks, screws, or rivets. Then after a pause she suggested tentatively they might be called "nails." So one realized there was a moment in the past when she first heard that the little pointed bits of iron were called "nails," and on to these were transferred affective thoughts and phantasies and deeds associated with her own nails. Hence the reason why she could not remember the word "nails."

An inhibition in connection with reading the daily paper was illuminated for me by a patient bewailing the fact repeatedly, "I have not read the paper this week. I don't know what has been happening. I haven't looked at the paper at all." During the course of the analytical hour her seemingly chance associations brought her to the fact that she was menstruating. Then the theme with which she opened came to my mind: "I have not *read* the paper. I don't know what has been happening." I realized then that the sound "red" will be first known by a tiny child in conjunction with a colour sensation, and that the later use of "read" as the past tense or past participle of "read" will carry with it also its first significance, Thus I was put on the track of an actual experience, namely that of seeing menstrual blood in a lavatory (paper) when the sight had aroused anxiety. So we can understand a deeper significance in "I don't know what is happening in the world."

33

A patient told me he dreamt of " *a meal at which a sirloin of beef was being carved.*" Brought up in a specific environment and at a time when in such households the courtesy term " sir " was in common usage, I had little doubt that a " sirloin " once meant for him the " loin of a sir."

If the patient dreams of the sea not only will water be a significant element but it is useful to remember that " see " and " sea " have the same sound and the theme of looking will also be important. One may assume because of one's knowledge of symbols that *a pier* in a dream will signify the phallus. But I find that one often gets into touch with human experience more quickly if one remembers that " pier " and " peer " sound alike, that " peer " means " look " and that " piers " are to be found at the seaside where opportunities of looking and seeing are many.

" *In my dream the meal was all over and I felt angry,*" said a patient. She went on to elaborate thus: " One would feel upset if one wanted to go on eating because one was hungry." The clue to the dream lay in the patient's substitution of " upset " for " all over," when she elaborated the dream. Infantile emotional " upsets " are accompanied by concrete happenings.

" Sandwich " is an interesting word. It is sometimes useful as referring to a time when the child lay between its parents. A fish-paste sandwich I have found can indicate what the child placed between its parents. To eat a sandwich can symbolize the incorporation of both parents. But I have found the " sandwich " in a dream is adequately explained only when associations have

34

brought memories of the sands on the seashore. The word " wich " (which) has represented not only the query concerning the genitals, the difference between girl and boy, but also the potentialities of the development of the " witch " psychology in the little girl.

An interesting dream told to me by a patient was accompanied by great anxiety "*lest bats in a lavatory pan over which she wanted to sit should fly into her anus.* My interest at the moment is not the symbolism of the phantasy but the fact that from associations to the dream it was possible to date the phantasy in connection with a definite illness. At the time of an illness from influenza I gathered that the patient was suffering also from an anxiety neurosis. Her conscious dread at that time was of being splashed by the water while sitting on the lavatory seat. She was suffering from " influenza." The word being then apparently unknown, the child only understood the sound of " flu " (flew). Hence " influenza " became the vehicle of her unconscious phantasy. In the dream there is the fear lest " bats " should fly into her anus; we can infer therefore that " enza " signified for the child " bats," and that associated with " bats " were frightening unconscious phantasies.

In families where children have a religious upbringing the word " hymn " must primarily designate a man. A patient at the age of sixteen became devoted to Tennyson's " In Memoriam." A dream revealed that the format of the poem, its arrangement into groups of stanzas, had unconsciously become associated with the lay-out of a hymn-book. The hymn of childhood was praise of the beloved good father. The " In Memoriam " of adolescence was the praise of a good lost object and thereby represented the psychical retention of that good object.

A " running " figure in a dream can always be interpreted as symbolical of urinary experiences which precede the child's ability to run on its own legs, the bodily motion or " movement " that long antedates spatial movement. When a patient expresses anxiety concerning his love affairs by repeating the phrase " falling in love " one finds a key to a wealth of phantasy by treating the phrase " falling in " as a dread of an actual " falling into." Should a bird called a " swallow " appear in a dream one may remember that the dreamer heard the word " swallow " in the first place connected with food. The word " stroke " has many significances. It has both a loving and fierce meaning. I have had three patients who in early childhood had direct experience of people having " strokes." One patient had sunstroke herself, the other two had ocular experience of adults stricken by sudden seizures. In each case the word " stroke " was laden with affective meaning. In one, an early displacement of affect was made on to " up-strokes " and " down-strokes " in early writing lessons, thus making the acquisition of writing a retarded painful accomplishment. I have known writing to be retarded too because of the term " pot-hooks " employed in the teaching of writing.

A patient after a dream concerning raspberries remembered vomiting as a child after he had eaten raspberries. The clue to understanding, apart from

36

one's deductions through analytic experience, came in the information that raspberries were called " rasps " at home. The word " rasp " brought several memories such as the " feel " of the cat's tongue, the cat's fur rubbed the wrong way, the " feel " of the implement called a " rasp," and finally the fact of the " hairs " on the raspberry itself. From these associations it was not difficult to understand the unconscious phantasy associated with the " rasps " that caused the child to vomit. I have had corroboration from several patients that a child interprets the phrase " furred tongue " quite literally.

The presence of a " see-saw " in a dream will lead one direct to a masturbation theme because of the bodily movement implied, but a " see-saw " will denote also a connection between masturbation and sight which may be of importance in the specific sexual history. Here is another interesting insight into phantasy formation. A child gradually apprehended that his father went into the city every day because he was a " stockbroker." The first meaning this term had for him was that his father was engaged in " breaking stock." Then the child heard his father talk of " widows' insurance." He did not know what a " widow " was. The nearest meaning that he could supply was " window," so the logical deduction from his own range of facts was that his father's work in the city was breaking windows. When " widow " was understood to be a woman the unconscious phantasy was still further reinforced.

If events in a dream take place in a drawing-room, or a with-drawing-room we may expect

" drawing " to be possibly of importance. The first accessible significance will often be that of drawing with pen, pencil or crayon, but finally we can rely upon bodily processes revealing the ultimate meaning of the dream, such as sucking from, or out of. One gets further help from even concrete terms by not remaining satisfied with the first one offered.

The names of places selected by the dream as appropriate for the drama enacted may sometimes be helpful towards its elucidation. Bournemouth, Barmouth, Wales, Maidenhead, Virginia Water, Hyde Park Corner, Chile, Spion Kop, Lyons' Corner House, Covent Garden, are a few typical examples of such place names.

Names, both Christian and surname, are useful in the same way, sometimes directly as given in the manifest content, sometimes indirectly as the opposite of the manifest content. The name " Sharpe," for instance, is often indicated in a dream by a " flat " or a " block of flats." " Mr. Seymour," " Mr. Attwater," " Mrs. Payne," are further examples of definite names which have been useful in the interpretation of specific dreams.

The dream then has a twofold value; it is the key to the understanding of unconscious phantasy and it is the key to the storehouse of memory and experience. The unconscious wish and phantasy have at their disposal all experiences from infancy. As an approach to the mechanisms that make the manifest dream out of latent thoughts and the unconscious store of experience and impulse I have detailed the principles and devices employed by poetic diction, since these principles bear so directly

38

the impress of the same origin as dream mechanisms. I have indicated the help to be obtained in elucidating dreams from the simple fact that the bridges of thought are crossed and re-crossed by names, that the basis of language is implied metaphor and that we all learned our mother tongue phonetically.

CHAPTER II

Mechanisms of Dream Formation

1. THE LAW OF CONDENSATION.
   (a) The underlying psychic conflict and its power of selecting appropriate psychical material.
   (b) Importance of this law of condensation in all mental activity.
   (c) The value of elaboration of the condensation.

2. DISPLACEMENT.
   The different methods of displacement with illustrative material.

3. SYMBOLIZATION.
   (a) Typical and individual symbols.
   (b) Symbols in the service of hate and love impulses.

4. DRAMATIZATION.
   Play, dreams and drama. Dreams the attempt within the psyche to project and master anxiety.

5. SECONDARY ELABORATION.

THE transformation of latent into manifest dream content is brought about by specific mechanisms. Freud names them condensation, displacement, dramatization, symbolization and secondary elaboration. We will now consider each mechanism in further detail.

CONDENSATION

A dream will not only evoke associations to present-day events and emotions but will also recall events, phantasies and emotions belonging to differing times and circumstances in the past. Here is a simple example: A man dreamt that *he saw a light-ship that had a walrus as a figure-head.* The associations evoked by the dream brought first of all to mind an experience of a rough journey by sea that he had made the preceding week-end. On that voyage he had seen actual lightships and lifebuoys. These seen during storm had given a fantastic impression as the rough tides swept over them. They were like heads and the water poured out of their nostrils. The perils of navigation in a stretch of water where sand-banks were numerous were the first thoughts of the patient. He had good reason to be glad during that rough passage that he knew the navigation map by heart, since he was the captain of the vessel.

The specific detail of " walrus " recalled to his mind a chart which used to hang on his nursery wall. This chart had on it illustrations of different animals, one of which he remembered clearly as a walrus. It had two large tusks. This chart was mounted on rollers in the same way as geographical maps were, so that maps and charts thus became associated in the child's mind. The pictured walrus had also its living counterpart. The children in the nursery called an old woman servant of the family " the walrus." She had two large canine teeth, which, so the nursery legend went, kept on growing, and she had to visit the dentist periodically to have them sawn off. The external danger the patient had proved he could meet and survive was the negotiation of the " mouth " of the Thames in a storm.

I have not given here an interpretation of the dream. There were other elements in it in addition to the above, but I have illustrated how in the one detail of the " walrus " there were condensed memories of present-day lightships and buoys, present-day navigation maps, schoolroom wall maps, the chart of the pictured animals on the wall, and the old servant nicknamed " the walrus "!

Latent meanings still unknown are implicit. One notices, for instance, the repetition of the " wall " element in wall-map, wall-chart, walrus. What is the significance of " figure-head " ? It is evident that a wealth of latent meaning was still unexplored in this analytical hour.

All that a patient says during one session in which a dream is related will not represent the latent thoughts that have contributed to the manifest content. It is the task of the analyst to sift, to correlate, to recognize recurring themes, the turning from these as resistance develops, and the returning to them after digressions.

The condensation of a mass of latent thoughts, memories and phantasies in a dream can be illustrated by a concrete image. Suppose that a hundred different small objects made of different materials lie on a table. If a magnet is drawn through them in all directions every article made of iron will be picked up by the magnet. So one may think of any dynamic unconscious interest as a magnet which will gather together out of the whole reservoir of past and present-day experiences just those particular ones that are pertinent to that magnet. Such experiences will extend from present-day situations to infancy if it were possible to find them.

42

This mechanism of condensation that Freud discovered in dream formation has a further validity and import. It is not only a feature of dream activity, but it is inseparable from all mental functioning, conscious and unconscious alike.

I will illustrate my meaning first from a demonstrable example drawn from another sphere of mental activity. It is the counterpart of the scientific discovery of law. The *Rime of the Ancient Mariner*, written by Coleridge, came into being in a short time almost as flawless in language and conception as we have it extant to-day. Thanks to a student of Coleridge's works,[1] John Livingston Lowes, and to the fact that Coleridge left behind him notes of the works he read so omnivorously, one is able to trace, not the activity that urged the theme, but the law of condensation that brought about the format, the setting of the theme. The whole poem is an immense condensation into one unity of a thousand pictorial images and of feeling tones from dozens of books that Coleridge had read. This unity was brought about by the psychical mechanism of condensation, obedient to the magnet of unconscious interest, the source of all intellectual activity. The rapidity of composition of this poem illustrates the amazing operations of this law of condensation below the level of consciousness. We see the same psychical processes at work in the case of the scientist. The dynamics of the intellectual activity is in the driving interest of the latent thoughts directed to the observation of some range of external phenomena. From thousands of particularities the scientist at last reveals a

[1] John Livingston Lowes. *The Road to Xanadu.* 1927.

theory or a truth concerning the external universe and in this final outcome of his work the mechanism of condensation has played a part as it does in the work of a poet. Hence my statement that Freud's discovery is of greater import even than we thought at first. It is an integral process in all mental functioning, unconscious and conscious.

I should like next to point out further conclusions that follow on this realization. Scientific theories concerning the nature and operation of the external universe are from time to time abandoned or modified or changed. This is because facts not previously known have to be recognized which then may make the former conclusions invalid or necessitate a restatement. The greater the range of observable data the more it is possible for valid inferences to be drawn. The range of facts that any given person can observe is limited, but the special limitation that is pertinent at the moment both to observation of facts and acceptance of them is the one due to emotional difficulties. Conclusions are drawn and deductions made from the facts that are available to him, not from the facts that are in reality available, but from the selection he makes. In that selection, the omissions will be as significant as those included, just as in the scientist's formulation, the non-observed data may eventually falsify his conclusions. That is, the very facts observed can lead to false inferences.

The bearing that this has on the theme of condensation is important in this way. In a dream we are presented with the condensation of latent thoughts, memories and experiences. By exploration of the latent thoughts, we bring to consciousness some part of an interrelated chain of phantasies, experiences, emotions. The evocation of memory and of emotion in actual experience during analysis, brings to consciousness the wrong deductions that have been made and so also the facts of reality we were not able to know or accept. The ego, that is, extends its boundaries. The result of this is that the unconscious mechanism of condensation can work over a greater range of experience and thus our intellectual activities become less dominated by a subjective selection of data and we are not driven to hasty formulation dictated by unconscious wishes and fears.

DISPLACEMENT

Displacement in a dream is accomplished by putting an element in the foreground of interest in the manifest content which will be of least significance when the latent thoughts to the dream are evoked. On the other hand an insignificant detail in the manifest content may lead to the most important latent thoughts. The affect in the dream may likewise accompany the least important dream thought, while dream thoughts powerfully affective may be represented in the manifest content of the dream by elements of feeble affective tone. Freud terms this the " transvaluation of all values."

Displacement accounts for the frequent bizarre effect of a dream when there is incongruity between the intensity of affect and the intellectual content.

I will give you two or three examples of dreams to illustrate the mechanisms of displacement. A dreamer related the following: "*I was on the beach at the place called X. Apparently I was going to swim.*" The dream had a pleasant feeling tone. During the analysis many memories concerning the place X were recalled and the gist of all of them was that the patient was an excellent swimmer. During the narration of these visits to X he said at intervals "X is on the east side of the bay." On the third repetition of this fact I said, "Why do you repeat X is on the east side ? Do you know the west side ? " After a pause he told me that a place called Y was on the west side of the bay but that he was quite young when the family went to Y and that he could not swim at that time. Then I learned that he was five years of age when he first went there. He then remembered an important fact in connection with Y. Two dead bodies were washed ashore while he was on the beach.

The displacement from west to east achieves the following: In the manifest dream there is no uncomfortable feeling, for he is an accomplished swimmer and will not drown. Exhibitionism is legitimate in the sublimated form of swimming. The latent thoughts revealed disturbing memories of dead bodies. At that time he could not swim. These memories brought to the patient's mind a period of bed-wetting when he was a child. The urethral phantasies of aggression associated with bed-wetting were ultimately linked with his own fears of drowning.

Here is another type of displacement. The dreamer awoke with great pleasure repeating the lines: "*And give to airy nothings a local habitation and a name.*" The awakened dreamer spent some minutes meditating on this quotation and then realized the latent thoughts; the "local habitation" was the anus and the airy nothings were "wind." The affective memory, however, during analysis was the word "fart," and this caused as much shame in uttering as the quoted lines had given pleasure. Such displacement is called "euphemism" in poetic diction. The further analysis of the word "fart" revealed still earlier displacement. She remembered as a child of five saying the Lord's Prayer aloud to her mother before going to bed. Her mother once interposed during the recital of this and requested her to repeat certain words again. The child repeated "Our Father which *chart* in heaven," and when told she was repeating it wrongly she found the correct words "Our Father which art" quite unintelligible. During the analysis the word "chart" evoked memories of the music notation printed on a long roll from which the pupils had a singing lesson. This was the music chart which she thought of in the prayer. "Art" conveyed no meaning. The analysis proved that the placing of the "ch" before "art" to make "chart," which word she understood, was also a defence against thinking of the forbidden word "fart" and the ideas that word conveyed. The word that was supplied by her, namely "chart," with the significance of singing gives us an example of the "return of the repressed," a sublimated interest in sound.

I am indebted to another patient for this interesting psychical experience. She woke up from this dream quite suddenly. "*I was standing in a street looking up at a window which was open. A woman was standing there. I was only able to see the woman's head and shoulders and the upper part of her body which was fully clothed.*" The patient, already acquainted with the theory of dreams, was interested in the sudden awakening and thought, " What can there be in a dream like this to make me wake ? " She fell asleep and again woke suddenly. This time she had further dreamt that she was inside the room where the woman was whom she had seen in the previous dream at the windows from the street. The dreamer, now a child, was on the floor, and she looked up and saw not the woman's head and shoulders and face from the front, but her back, and the body was naked; a repressed memory of a bedroom scene in early childhood. The spatial displacement by reversal in the first dream is here neatly demonstrated.

Displacement is in the second dream achieved by the two methods I illustrated when speaking of the figures of speech, metonymy and synecdoche. In metonymy an associated idea will represent the thing itself.

A patient dreamt *he was playing a game of bowls.* The significance of the game was found through the association of bowls with porridge, and the shape of these bowls suggested chambers and then the nursery pot with its contents of water and fæces. This mechanism was illustrated also in the dream where the dreamer was in anxiety concerning the slatey look of a new-born child. The " slatey " colour was an attribute standing for the slates themselves and in the dream it effected a displacement from the thing, namely the slate tombstone with which was associated the real affect.

Here is a dream illustrating intense affect connected with a seemingly unimportant element. The patient dreamt that she saw "*an ordinary black spotted woman's veil drawn over a knee.*" The patient awoke from this dream with a feeling of indescribable horror and loathing of the veil, and so great was the recoil from the manifest content that it was some time before she could bring herself to talk about it. The horrible phantasies were then found to be connected not with the veil but with what lay under the veil, the first series of memories being connected with her mother's legs, on which she remembered elastic stockings and her horror lest these swollen legs should burst. The point of the illustration is the displacement of affect on to the cover instead of the thing itself.

Here is a dream that caused a happy affect. The reason for this was the success of the displacements together with the superimposing of a happy memory over an unhappy one. The dream was: "*Wake up, wake up, wake up. This is the river Moldau. Here King Wenceslas lived, and this is the cherry tree that grew in Charles Dickens' garden.*" The "cherry tree" is an example of displacement. The patient remembered that she was swinging in a cherry tree when she was told that she had a new baby sister. *Wake up, wake up, wake up* fused together unhappy and happy memories of being awakened to pass water, and of the joyous waking on Christmas morning to find Christmas presents. The patient remembered the story of King Wenceslas as one in which a king went on a journey taking gifts to the poor. She spoke of Charles Dickens' *Christmas Carol* in which a miser had a change of heart and gave generously

49

to the needy. In the Christmas story itself she remembered the gift of the Christ child to the humble maiden Mary. So the dream wish emerged, the hope for the gift of a child. Deeper-lying urethral phantasies and bodily experiences were indicated, though in the specific session not elucidated. Such indications are forthcoming in the associations the patient made to the stimulus of the river Moldau. The word made her think successively of mould, iron mould and the stain left on a mattress when urine had soaked into it.

Displacement may be also secured by the method of substituting the part for the whole, which as a figure of speech is called "synecdoche." One example will suffice. A patient dreamt *that there appeared to be great excitement because a baby was expected. She knew that clothes were being prepared. She wanted to make her own gift too. She put into the drawer with the prepared clothes a pair of baby's slippers.* This dream as you will surmise brought memory and conjecture concerning the preparations made for her rival's appearance when she was a child. The first significance of the dream appeared when she remembered giving back to her little brother a pair of his red shoes she had envied and of which she wanted to deprive him. There followed the revelation of envy of his penis, and the desire to take it from him. Finally we had evidence of her rage when her mother was pregnant and her desire to take the baby from her mother's body. We see in the dream the mechanism of the part for whole, and of the things associated representing the thing itself, for example, shoes for feet, shoes for the penis, and finally shoes for the whole child. The manifest dream content of restoration reveals the underlying wish to take away the mother's child. I am here giving not a complete interpretation of the actual dream, but the stage reached during one session.

Displacement achieved by reversal I have illustrated by the dream of the woman seen at the window from the street, but all dreamers are not so obliging as to produce a second dream in which the truth is given, and one finds some types of reversal dreams difficult to elucidate.

Common reversal mechanisms consist in such devices as representing an incident occurring " outside " when all pertinent associations lead to the conclusion that the event must be located " inside." The " top " often represents displacement from the " bottom," and " over " from " under." The dream concerning the " head of a walrus " to which I have referred with the associations of the dangers of wind and water in navigation, indicated a phantasy concerning ultimately not the head at all but the lower bodily orifices, that is, a *figure-head*. Again although the actual manifest content gave the external appearance of the head, the really affective latent thoughts concerned the inside, not the outside, and in this instance the external reality of a rough and dangerous sea was the counterpart of the phantasies of anxiety concerning the dangerous interior of the body.

Dreams of the following type show an interesting form of displacement. " *I was climbing up some steps which were on the outside of a building and as I climbed the danger of falling became imminent as the steps began to give way.*" The meaning of such a dream is fairly obvious as the symbolism of masturbation, erection and detumescence. But it can also represent an actual babyhood experience of climbing when a "falling" of the contents from the inside of the body occurred.

In the dreams of patients with whom the problem of repressed homosexuality is of major importance reversals can be of a complicated pattern and not obvious in the manifest content of dreams at all. Here is such a dream. "*I was talking to a woman who told me she had had an illegitimate child by a man called 'Hughes' and she asked me if I was still prepared to marry her.*" The manifest content implies that the dreamer, a man, was the lover of the woman who had borne him an illegitimate child. One clue to this complicated dream problem was given within the first quarter of an hour of the session by repeated allusions to men who had turned theories upside down, such as " Epstein has turned old conceptions of art upside down." The concrete significance of the word "conception" linked with the phrase "upside down" led at once to a latent phantasy concerning anal birth. My interpretation of "Hughes" as "whose" led to the unconscious phantasy of the dreamer's own illegitimate birth, for he is "Hughes" in the dream. The dreamer in real life has a sensitive ear and was very resistant to this interpretation of unconscious punning.

Here is a dream that reveals the condensation of many bitter experiences in a simple displacement. "*I gave a ball of silver paper to old Dr. X.*" The silver paper brought to the patient's mind the coverings of chocolates. His mother used to eat the chocolate and the child collected the wrappings. Dr. X had attended the child since birth. Circumcision, operations on tonsils and adenoids occurred in the first five years. When the anæsthetic was given in the tonsil operation Dr. X said " I've some nice scent for you to smell." It proved to be nauseating and suffocating. On an occasion of a visit in early manhood to a dentist the patient gave the dentist a present saying " Here's a cigar." The dentist took it and found it collapsible. " You see," said the patient, " I gave him a dummy and he thought it was going to be a real present! "

SYMBOLISM

The chief method of distorting the latent thoughts is accomplished by symbolism. The difference between general symbolism to which I drew your attention in figures of speech, and symbolism in the strict sense of the word as used in psycho-analytic theory is that in the latter one member of the equation is in the unconscious mind. A simile says frankly this is like this, a metaphor is an identification of two knowns, but to understand the true symbolism of the unconscious one must find the repressed equivalent.

Psycho-analytic experience has shown that the ideas that are symbolized concern the fundamental basic factors of our actual existence, namely our own bodies, life, death and procreation. These fundamentals in relation to ourselves and the family of which we were a member, retain for us through life their original importance, and energy flows from them to all derivative ideas.

> Our first affections, our shadowy recollections
> Which be they what they may,
> Are yet the master light of all our day.

Symbolism occurs in one direction only, namely, from the unconscious mind, the symbols being the representation of the repressed unconscious content.

[1]Rank and Sachs comment on symbolism thus: " The prevalence of sexual meanings in symbolism is not to be explained merely by the fact that no other instinct has been as subjected to social suppression as the sexual one and is therefore extensively susceptible of and in need of indirect representation but also for the genesis of symbolism there is the phylogenetic fact that in primitive civilization an immense importance was attached to the sexual organs and functions." This states the evolutionary basis of symbolism.

The variation in meaning of symbols is exceedingly limited, a striking feature being the constancy in different fields of symbolism as illustrated in the myths of countries widely separated.

Jones's view is that symbolism has to be created afresh out of individual material and that stereotypy is due to the fact of the fundamental perennial interests of mankind. The individual has the choice out of a number of possible symbols or can, as Freud pointed out, represent an idea by a symbol that has not been used before.

[1] *Die Bedeutung der Psychoanalyse für die Giesteswissenschaften.*

All intensive work with children in England following the impetus given by Mrs. Klein's researches confirm the truth of Jones's view[1] made long before such research was possible. Each individual creates symbolism afresh, such symbols as he will originate being inseparable from his environment, as for example, ships for sailors, the plough for farmers, the aeroplane and stink bombs for modern town-dwellers. The truth about symbolism in this respect was once stated for me very simply years ago by a girl of fourteen who had written an essay on " Fairy Tales." She concluded it thus: " If all the fairy tales in all the world were destroyed to-morrow it would not matter, for in the heart of the child they spring eternal."

I will give some examples of such individual symbols. I found in one patient's associations an overwhelming choice of a fish-pond as his main method of symbolization. The fish themselves, the occupation of fishing, the different methods of catching fish were all pressed into the service of symbolization. The fish represented as occasion required, fæces, children, penis. The patient lived on an estate from infancy to adolescence in which there was a large fish-pond. Another patient I have runs a whole gamut of phantasy upon sailing boats. In this case from infancy to adolescence long periods of time were spent by the sea, and the symbolism most prevalent in the analysis is in terms of ships.

Another piece of individual symbolism I have come across was that of a weaver's loom and shuttle. The big four-square loom was equated with

[1] *Papers on Psycho-Analysis.* Chapter VII, page 154.

a bed, the flying shuttle with the penis, the thread with semen, the making of the material from the thread with a child. The adoption of this particular symbol dated from the first year of the patient's life. The facts were that in her first year she went with her parents on a visit to a great-aunt who lived in the country; father, mother and child slept in a four-poster bed. She was taken on this occasion and later in childhood many times to see the silk-weaving looms in this particular district. She remembered in later childhood how she was fascinated by the swift flinging of the shuttle. The man sitting at the loom bending over his work and flinging the shuttle took over completely in phantasy the significance of scenes witnessed in infancy in the four-poster bed.

Moreover to an extent I have not found in any other patient, thread, silk, cotton, string had a predominating significance. Her recurrent nightmare through childhood and adolescence was in connection with string. Thread is a very common symbol for milk, water and semen, but the exclusive choice of it in an analysis I would say was only possible when an external environment provided a special stimulus. There was not an operation relevant to this work of weaving that did not appear as symbolic of unconscious phantasies.

The shuttle symbolized the penis, the thread carried along by the shuttle symbolized the semen, and the woven material resulting from the work of the shuttle symbolized the child. The snapping of the thread in the shuttle, which in actual weaving caused a temporary cessation of work, symbolized castration.

56

A little way from the house where another patient lived for many years after his birth was a hill which half-way up its incline had a small but definite plateau. Although the actual experience of climbing on to this plateau came in late childhood yet in one dream this patient told me, it became clear that he had made this plateau a symbol of the parent's lap and had transferred an affective incident of his earlier childhood on to the plateau.

I had an interesting analytical experience in connection with a stereotyped dream symbol which suddenly made it real and fresh again. The dreamer was a woman of fifty. The dream was quite simple. " *I was in a train, it drew up at a platform and I got out, and then I saw others were on the platform who had got out of the carriages. I never saw them inside, I never saw them get out or get in.*" The feeling about the dream in consciousness was boredom. She remarked: " Why I should dream about a thing so uninteresting I do not know." She turned to other themes. About half-way through the hour she " chanced " on the theme of a cinema entertainment she had seen the night before. She became enthusiastic about " Mickey Mouse " and described how Mickey Mouse jumped into the giraffe's mouth. She said: " The long neck had a series of windows down it, and one could see Mickey all the time, you didn't lose sight of him, you saw him go in, and come out." My realization was that there is a moment when a child sees a train for the first time, a time when it is a new and exciting phenomenon. People get out whom the child never saw get in. At such a moment a train can become the symbol of the human body.

57

Stereotyped as symbols may be for us, they are yet the evidence of original interests in a new and exciting world without and within. These illustrations are given in support of the fact that though there is a fundamental uniformity in the wishes that are symbolized there is a choice of symbol for the individual which is created anew out of individual material.

DRAMATIZATION

The two dream mechanisms I have not yet illustrated are dramatization and the secondary elaboration. The dramatization, speaking roughly, is the representation in the manifest dream of an action or a situation which the dream mechanisms evolve from the latent thoughts. A film of moving pictures is projected on the screen of our private inner cinema. This dramatization is done predominantly by visual images, although auditory representation is sometimes present. Dramatization in dreams is the reversion to concrete image thinking as in the illustrations given in poetic diction. The dreamer may as himself take part in the drama, sometimes the experience is that of being an onlooker. When the dreamer is apparently only an onlooker, there is the subjective experience of witnessing an occurrence external to the self. The narrator of a dream will speak of the dream figures as if they were actual objective beings who acted and spoke thus in the dream. There is no awareness that the dream is the creation of the dreamer. Mrs. Klein[1] has pointed out how closely children's

[1] *The Psycho-Analysis of Children*, page 8

58

dreams resemble their play, and that in analysis children will act out elements that have appeared in their dreams. In play the child not only overcomes the painful reality, but is assisted in mastering its instinctual fears and internal dangers by projecting them into the outer world.

A displacement of instinctual and internal dangers into the outer world enables the child not only to master its fear of them but to be more fully prepared against them. Freud has spoken of the dream as the guardian of sleep. One is led to think that this dramatization in dreams is the subjective attempt within the psyche to project and master anxiety and control stimuli.

Drama is derived from the same material as the dream. Could we analyse a play in terms of the inner life of the dramatist, we should find the plot and all the characters taking part in it to be aspects of himself, projections of himself into imaginary characters. In historical drama the personages chosen are those on whom can be projected those rôles that are representative of the intra-psychical conflict in the mind of the author. The dream is the matrix from which art is developed. " We are such stuff as dreams are made of." The world of dreams is a stage world, where nightly " one man in his time plays many parts."

In child analysis, as Mrs. Klein has shown, the child plays its dream, develops apprehension, enacts rôles.[1] With adults the value of dream-analysis is that something of this same purpose is served by the exploration of it. The internal drama is objectified, the setting of the story is brought

[2] *Ibid.*, page 176

up to date, and within the analytical room the different rôles in the drama often shift more rapidly from analyst to patient, from patient to analyst than any quick-change artist could perform it.

The drama is subject in construction to the limiting conditions inherent in the art. The factor of time is one. It may be that the story presented in three hours on the stage would cover in reality many years. The drama may in itself be a tragedy, it may represent a series of catastrophes, and these of the most horrible type, and yet it may bring satisfaction and extreme pleasure as a " work of art." Art imposes its own inner laws upon the raw material of the story, and by such devices as beauty of language, the laws of meter, symmetry and balance produce a unity of creation within which discordances resolve into harmony.

One sees in some dreams a kind of abortive drama. The different dream-mechanisms attempt to make out of the raw material of conflicting forces, out of material that can present the history of many years in a single dream, a product that is something of a unity such as we get in the sublimation of drama, a balancing of forces and neutralization of affects. When this balance and neutralization is not achieved, the dream leaves a disagreeable affect or anxiety disrupts it in a way similar to that which we experience when the art in a real drama is imperfect, leaving our emotions stirred either too painfully or not cathected as a whole.

I will give a few simple examples of dramatization illustrating the allocation of different rôles to personizations that represent the conflicting parts of the psyche. A patient dreamt that *she stood by a grave with her younger sister. The younger sister was weeping copiously and the dreamer scolded her for being sentimental.* The patient told me that the grave *was bordered by shrubs of daphne*, and as her sister's name was Daphne, it was clearly Daphne who was buried there. The desperate attempt to deal with the death wish was evinced by the actual presence in the dream of the sister herself. Again it was evinced by the attempt to convey to the sister both the wish for her to be out of the way and to silence the sister's grief at this wish. The wish is also dealt with by an identification with the younger sister herself, for the patient's associations revealed that she had on some occasion criticized herself for being sentimental when she had given a marked exhibition of grief on the death of a schoolgirl whom she knew but slightly. Note again that the grave was bordered by shrubs of daphne, alive and blooming, which fact tells us in this much-overdetermined dream of the magical fulfilment not only of death wish but of wish and power to bring to life again.

Here is an example of another type. The patient reported this dream: " *A friend came to me and said:* ' *How is the cockatoo these days?* ' *I knew somehow my friend was referring to a person and not to a bird. I said in my dream:* ' *Whom do you mean? I don't understand.* ' *He replied:* ' *Your analyst of course.* ' *Whereupon said the dreamer:* ' *I was very shocked and scolded him and said I never spoke or thought of my analyst like that.*" Further analysis of this dream led to more significant revelations than that of a reference to calling the analyst a cockatoo, but the dream as it stands illustrates very simply not only the dramatization of the different parts of the psyche as different personalities but also shows a neat way of expressing both impulse and censorship.

During the process of bringing to light the repressed memories and phantasies during analysis dreams will actively allocate the rôles between analyst and patient in terms of a current conflict. An interpretation for the first time of masturbation phantasies for example may be followed by dreams in which the patient severely reprimands a person (the analyst disguised) for speaking of forbidden things. Here the rôles of Id and Super-ego are reversed, the patient taking over the super-ego activity and the analyst representing the forbidden sexual activities.

One of the most interesting and obscure dreams I have been told illustrates very well the fact that in the dramatization of the dream there is an effort at restoring or gaining control of stimuli by projection. Freud regards the origins of projection as a " shaping of behaviour towards such excitation as bring with them an overplus of pain. There will be a tendency to regard them as though they were acting not from within but from without in order for it to be possible to apply against them the defensive measures of the barrier against them." Two dreams I had from an adult patient concerned themselves *with a house farther down the street from which he lived.* He developed in the dream an anxiety concerning *the happenings in this distant upper room and thought he heard a cry.* From the associations that were evoked coupled with the fact that the patient had sudden sensations in the ears I concluded that this dream represented the projection on to another house of a traumatic occurrence of which the patient had no actual memory, namely an operation on the ear when he was a tiny child. In this dream the occurrence took place outside himself, the cry of another external person reached his ears. But the actual ear sensation during the hour and the patient's dramatic movements of his hands accompanied by the words " I feel I want to say ' Go away, go away,' " made me feel very confident we had reached a representation of a trauma in very early childhood, even though there was no actual memory of it.

SECONDARY ELABORATION

Secondary elaboration is a mechanism which achieves a congruous and related story out of the multifarious latent thoughts. It differs from the other dream mechanisms in that it arises from more conscious levels of the mind. The latent thoughts and wishes disguised by the processes of condensation, displacement and symbolization are moulded by mental activity nearer consciousness into the semblance of a logical story. Moreover the dream thoughts find in the preconscious mind material which can well be used in the final evasion of the censorship before the dream reaches consciousness. I will give you two illustrations of this. You will remember I spoke of a patient who awoke with a great feeling of pleasure and found herself saying: " And give to airy nothings a local habitation and a name." She remembered no actual dream for the latent dream thoughts had found in the preconscious mind the perfect vehicle in the form of a stored fragment of poetry. Free associations made to this fragment as if it had been a dream soon revealed the latent thoughts which brought affect of a less pleasurable kind.

I relate in Chapter VI a dream concerning " a wizard." The preconscious material utilized by the latent dream thoughts consisted of memories of fairy tales about wizards read in childhood and pictures remembered from these same books. The patient had no difficulty in giving the details of these stories but considerable difficulty was experienced in telling me the association of " bogy " that came to his mind for it recalled an incident of the night before which he would rather have forgotten. In its turn the association of " bogy " revealed phantasies concerning his father. The dream related in this chapter beginning " Wake up, wake up, this is the river Moldau; here King Wenceslas lived and this is the cherry tree that grew in Charles Dickens' garden " is interesting from the point of view of secondary elaboration. The seeming congruity is only just achieved and the disparate elements are easily detected.

Secondary elaboration attempts to bring the dream into harmony with conscious mental processes, to modify, make it comprehensible and acceptable to consciousness. Ernest Jones[1] speaks of it as being closely allied to the process known as rationalization.

The secondary elaboration of a dream, the welding together into a congruous whole of disparate elements is the analogue in the unconscious mind

[1] *Papers on Psycho-Analysis.* Chapter VII, page 204.

of the activity that occurs nearer conscious levels in the mind of a creator. The artist *consciously* participates in the psychical activity that culminates in a work of art. The secondary elaboration of a dream is achieved below consciousness. The conscious ego has taken no part in it.

CHAPTER III

EVALUATION OF DREAMS IN PSYCHO-ANALYTIC PRACTICE

1. Dream interpretation the corner-stone of psycho-analytic technique.
2. The value of the dream for the analyst.
3. The value of exploration of the preconscious with reference to the work of Freud and Jones.
4. The latent content is the clue to the wish-fulfilment.
5. Convenience dreams.
6. Illustrations of the value of dreams in addition to that of latent content.

FREUD's *Interpretation of Dreams* was the first text-book for psycho-analysts. His discovery of the unconscious mind placed in the foreground of interest the significance of dreams. Psycho-analytic technique in the early days of the therapy directed the patient's attention to them during the analytical hour almost to the exclusion of other topics in which the patient might be interested. " Free association " sometimes meant in practice free association to dreams, and a patient who insisted upon dwelling upon other things was at times regarded as showing " resistance " to analysis. The technique of analysis was almost synonymous with the technique of dream interpretation. Every dream was eagerly exploited as the one and only way into the unconscious mind and a patient who did not dream presented a great problem to the analyst for whom the sole key was the dream.

We know that dreams are not indispensable. We treat all that is said and done during the analytical hour as significant and our problem is to find the precise significance.

One wonders sometimes if the pendulum has swung to the opposite extreme, and if instead of an over-valuation of dreams as a means of analysing a patient we are not in some danger of under-valuation. We may need to take stock again of the value of dreams, and to make an assessment concerning dreams in general.

We must remember that the interpretation of dreams stands as the corner-stone of psycho-analysis, and that mainly by such interpretation psycho-analysis first earned by the cures achieved, adherents to the new therapy. The dream still remains I believe an important and almost indispensable means of understanding unconscious psychical conflicts.

I will give first some advantages the analyst himself stands to gain by understanding a patient's dreams. Dreams serve as a kind of reference in analytic work. We can gauge by dreams, if we can interpret them, how true or wide of the mark are our interpretations of the patient's general run of associations, of his gestures or behaviour. We eventually either get corroborations of our interpretations or we find that the patient's dreams indicate that we are not grasping the trend of affairs. I do not mean that we can understand every dream recounted by the patient nor can we follow up clearly the psychical problems from one dream to the next continuously. If we could see the end from the beginning we should be as gods. I mean that at intervals we shall find dreams being told to us that show our analytic interpretations are accurate since they will be followed by dreams that corroborate and pursue and unfold further material of the relevant theme. Here is an example of the process I mean. A patient noticed during an hour's analysis some catkins in a vase. She spoke of the pollen falling from them and then of the prodigality of nature. Her thoughts were " tuned in," so to speak, to one idea, that of profusion and generosity. The people who came to her mind were all of one type, generous with money, with ideas, with affection. The analyst said: " There was surely a time when you thought of your father as a generous giver. You seem to have thought of him as having abundance of good things which he gave generously, so much so he could afford not to care if there was waste." To this the patient replied incredulously, " But my father as long as I can remember only gave me two presents." The analyst replied, " That's as far back as you can remember, but you don't remember earlier than four years of age, do you ? " The patient agreed. The next day the patient told a dream in which " running water " was the main element. This evoked associations leading to her memory of the ecstasy she felt on first seeing a waterfall. The inference was drawn that she had first experienced this kind of excitement on seeing her father's penis while he was urinating. During the hour there suddenly came to the patient a vision of hanging fruit, clustered pears she thought, and finally she herself volunteered that this picture must be a representation of her father's genitals seen in infancy

68

when primitive oral desires hallucinate fulfilment from shapes that resemble the breast and nipple. This illustrates the value of the dream from the analyst's point of view, namely as a kind of touchstone of the validity of interpretation. Dreams will tell us whether we are really in touch with the unconscious mind of the patient. There are dreams we can only partially interpret in the light of the material given. We have only a partial understanding of an unfolding situation. There are other dreams which confirm and elaborate the accurate interpretations we have given. From this point of view, for grip of his own work, the dream is invaluable for the analyst.

I will give another type of value we gain from dreams. One needs to re-read at times the dream analyses detailed by Freud and Jones in their expositions of dreams. These analyses are classical examples of the bringing to light of the emotional situations of the current day and present-day stimuli. Beyond certain affective situations Freud thought fit to reveal in connection with his own childhood these dreams do not supply us with a great deal of either memory material nor of deep-seated unconscious phantasy. Neither could we expect it. What Freud has shown in a way unsurpassable is the immense ramification of preconscious thoughts, so illustrating the distorting mechanisms of condensation, displacement, symbolization and dramatization, for the purpose of psychic ease in wish-fulfilment.

Freud's actual analyses of dreams give us on the massive scale the value of the associations to a dream as a means of understanding the present-day emotional situations and conflicts in terms of the present-day events. They are examples of searching self-analysis of the pre-conscious, such as a fearless mind can undertake when there is enough self-knowledge to draw inferences from the material. These dreams draw our attention to one value of the dream, namely an investigation by free association of the significant present-day stimuli and the present-day setting of conflict and emotion. Without the present-day setting we do not and cannot comprehend the unity of the psychical life. We may know by interpretation of dream symbolism that a woman unconsciously is punishing herself for the wish to deprive her mother of children, or for the belief that omnipotently she brought about the death of her small brother at the age of two, but it is the exploration of the dream in terms of the pre-conscious and conscious mind that will give us just how this primitive wish, belief and guilt feeling work out in present-day life itself and, during the analysis, in terms of transference to the analyst.

Given a woman of fifty, married, and with grown-up children, the dominance of this unconscious conflict will have resulted in specific present-day situations and present-day thinking. More than half a lifetime of psychical building has been done in connection with this major core of the long past. Not by the mere magic of interpretation alone shall we alter the patient's psychical orientation, an interpretation which was possible for the analyst to make in the case of this woman in the first week of analysis. The analyst must illustrate this past still living in the present, the past that cannot be left behind. We can do this only by seeing people of the present day in the rôles of past imagoes, by seeing what are the present-day equivalents of past situations and realize the denouéments that are forever being reached. So in this particular patient the problem revealed itself in terms of houses first of all. Over a period of years her husband had secured house after house for her, always with the one result that her interest gradually waned, she finally disliked her home and decided they must leave it. She then had a prolonged holiday after which they made a fresh start. One factor alone is quite inadequate to explain this woman's unrest but one factor was undoubtedly the self-punishment of turning herself out of her house to make amends for the wish and the belief that she had turned her brother out. My point at the moment is that the dream is a means of exploring the pre-conscious which together with its correlation with the conscious present-day settings of emotion and conflict will also include the past conflicts brought up to date. By this means, whether in transference or in the wider-flung life of the patient in all activities, we can estimate how far repressed memories and unconscious conflicts are contributing an untoward influence upon present-day life and conduct.

I have found dreams an invaluable clue to a repressed major traumatic situation which an adult patient was compelled continually to re-stage again in terms of his current life in order to bring about magically both the same and a different outcome from the original. Such dramatization in real life is of constant occurrence. It may be innocuous when not of a massive type having no untoward effect on the person's life in reality. For example,

I know of a patient who for years never knew the reason why a bath taken during the day-time gave her a sense of well-being that no morning or evening bath afforded her. We found in the course of analysis that as a child of five she had been left to her own devices one afternoon and possessed of a jar of paste for sticking scraps in an album she had not only pasted in the scraps but had then proceeded to cover the furniture in the room and finally herself with the sticky paste. Her father on his return had smacked her hands, the first time he had physically punished her. The escapade was followed not only by a washing of the furniture but she herself was bathed. Clean and tidy once more the child saw her father again, was forgiven and kissed. The afternoon bath for the patient of forty still brought a feeling of absolution that was greater than mere cleanliness. Nor, I may add, did the knowledge she gained of the significance of her unconscious dramatization lessen her satisfaction in an afternoon bath. This is a minor and innocuous example of dramatization. More serious types occur. When such dramatization constitutes in itself the re-enacting of the dissociated traumatic occurrence, dreams can be an important means of the resuscitation of the prototype of the dramatization. Here is such a dream which after a long baffling analysis brought me insight concerning the problem the patient was compelled to dramatize. Although the interpretation brought no direct conviction to the patient and no recovered memory it yet had the effect of making the actual dramatizations that subsequently took place less fraught with serious consequences than former ones. The dream ran thus: " *I said good-bye to G. and sent her away and then I turned to you to embrace you* [i.e. the analyst] *and said good-bye. But I was standing on stilts and my dilemma was that if I let go my hand on the stilts to bend forward to kiss you it would mean my legs would give way and I should fall.*" From the associations given I was able to make the interpretation that in the dream the analyst represented the patient when a child and the patient in the dream represented a grand-parent. The patient had been told, but had no active memory, of an incident that occurred when she was two years of age. The grandparent was bending down to kiss the child when he collapsed from a seizure from which he died. I cannot enter here into all the fatalistic phantasies that sub-sequently were inseparable from the love impulses of this child. My purpose is to tell you that this dream gave the first satisfactory clue to the repeated dilemmas the patient unconsciously brought about which were an attempt to deal with the early trauma bound up with the deepest anxieties, for this trauma was a sudden dramatic loss by death of a good object—not a phantasied loss only.

I have spoken of the value of dreams as the touchstone by means of which the analyst can gauge how near he is to following the movements of the unconscious mind; that is, he will get cor-roboration and further elaboration following his interpretation.

I have spoken of the value of exploring the pre-conscious as giving us the modern setting in which the long past is still played out, the modern persons in the old drama, the modern substitutes in present-day situations moulded on the past, the way in which guilt is assuaged in present-day terms, or in which old rebellions are staged again.

My next evaluation of dreams is in the matter of transference. Again, I think the dream is a touch-stone with regard to the accuracy of interpretation of the transference. The analyst, by the help of dreams, can keep in close touch with what actually is being transferred unconsciously on to him and from whom transferred. The analyst needs to preserve objectivity if the patient is to gain it in this matter. Only by the analysis of the transference do we ultimately analyse the past in the present and so ultimately the unconscious conflicts. The dream par excellence with its associations gives us the bridge between the present and the past, just as for the time being the analyst is the person on to whom the problems in the unconscious mind are trans-ferred. It is to this aspect of transference the analyst must adhere, and I know of no corrective like dreams to illuminate the fact that it is the infantile elements of development that are thus worked out in transference on to the analyst. We shall not be tempted to look upon the positive transference to ourselves as the equivalent of the love-life of a full personality, but as the transferred affects of a conflict within the psyche. Patients at various stages will of course equate their feelings for the analyst as being those of the mature adult. But the analyst if he is to deliver over the patient to a real love life must never lose sight of the fact that the remote secluded hour of analysis is part of the total phantasy that is being worked out and understood. The dream is the great help and corrective since in the dream we can see what is being transferred, what situation is being enacted, what rôle is being thrust on to the analyst, what past affective situation is being re-staged.

This leads me directly to what may be called the cardinal rule in dream analysis. There are many exceptions to this rule, but I believe there are more pitfalls for the analyst in neglecting the cardinal rule than there are in neglecting the many exceptions. This cardinal rule is that the meaning of a dream is ascertained by analysing the manifest content into its latent thoughts. The first impulse in connection with any dream is to try to interpret its meaning as it is given in the manifest content, and I believe this impulse has to be checked as much by the analyst in himself as in the patient. The understanding of the dream as a wish-fulfilment is only reached in this way. We, as well as patients, may say of the manifest content of a dream " but this cannot possibly be a wish." To find the wishes that are represented we must know the latent thoughts, and along with those (which may represent opposing wishes) we must include those psychical forces that bring about displacement and seeming congruity. To give the idea that all dreams are simple wish-fulfilments as presented in their manifest content is to give that partial truth which leads as much astray as a lie.

Here is a simple example of an anxiety dream. To say the dream as it stands is a wish-fulfilment is manifestly absurd. " *A man is acting for the screen. He is to recite certain lines of the play. The photographers and voice recorders are there. At the critical moment the actor forgets his lines. Time and again he makes the*

75

attempt with no result. Rolls of film must have been spoilt." The dreamer had great anxiety watching the actor fail at these critical moments.

It is only when one knows the latent content that one realizes the conflict of wishes represented in such a dream. The photographers and voice recorders cannot get the actor to perform although they are all assembled for that purpose. He forgets his lines. The anxiety of the dreamer is, in the manifest content, caused by the fact that he can say nothing when everyone is waiting for him to do so. The actual infantile situation revealed by the associations was that the dreamer was once the onlooker when his parents were " operating " together. The baby was the original photographer and recorder and he stopped the parents in the " act " by noise. The baby did not forget his lines! The original anxiety was connected with an actual doing, not with abstention from activity at the critical moment. It is always helpful to remember that original anxieties regarding our impulse life are concerned with what we did or wished to do, not with our sins of omission. The " return of the repressed " is given in the dream by the element " rolls of film must have been wasted " telling us by the device of metonymy, of a huge amount of fæcal matter the baby was able to pass at that moment.

Illustrated in this dream are some of the profoundest activities of the psyche. We have the recording of sight and sound by the infant and the incorporation by the senses of sight and hearing of the primal scene. We have evidence of this incorporated scene by its projection into the dream dramatization.

The modern invention of the screen of the cinema is pressed into service as the appropriate symbol, the screen being the modern external device corresponding to the internal dream picture mechanism.

The original onlooker becomes the active doer, drawing attention to himself, not in articulate words, but by inference from the wasted rolls to the one thing he could do, namely make a mess and a noise that brought the operators to a standstill. Moreover, by displacement of affect, of counter-wish against the original wish, by the dream work which attempts to resolve anxiety there is presented in miniature the conflict of desires.

The cardinal rule is to analyse the manifest dream into its latent elements. One finds in transference dreams particularly that patients will attempt to interpret the dream from its manifest content. There is often a marked resistance to submitting such dreams to analysis, that is of treating the elements separately and unearthing the infantile situation and finding the figure for whom the analyst is a proxy. When a strong positive or negative transference is in full swing a dream may so gather up the infantile longings and so strongly picture them with regard to the analyst that the manifest dream content is taken almost as a reality. The reason for this is often due to the fact that in the dream there is embedded a bit of childhood reality not remembered in consciousness, and unknown to the patient this submerged experience is being relieved. Again the important thing is to find the latent thoughts, and to track down the real experience. In the analysis of transference dreams this is vitally important. A patient will often say: " *Well, I dreamt about you*

77

last night, and you were doing so and so, or this and that happened." I find in such transference dreams the patient is particularly anxious to interpret the dream as a whole, and I am inclined to think that the analyst too may be more often tempted to consider manifest content rather than the latent one in such types of dreams. These above all must be explored for the repressed thoughts, phantasies and memories. Here is an example in illustration of my argument. "*I dreamt you were angry with me and would not forgive me.*" The patient who related this dream could not for a time rid herself of the conviction that the analyst was in reality angry with her. Only by the analyst's close following on of the work of the previous day's analysis did there emerge the memory of putting the paste over the furniture, an incident to which I referred in illustrating dramatization. The fact was that the child was angry with her father. In the analysis the affective projection on the analyst came first. " You are angry with me and won't forgive me." The psychical truth was " I am angry with you and won't forgive you," which was the real significance of the childhood escapade.

I find that short compact dreams also are apt to be taken at the valuation of the manifest content and interpreted often by the patient off-hand and dismissed with satisfaction. For example, a man patient says, "*I dreamt I was having successful intercourse with X.*" He goes on to say: " I told you I met her the other day and how pretty and attractive I thought she was." He comments further, " A very natural dream, and it is easy to see a wish-fulfilment." This is a good example of what I mean by the urge to interpret the manifest content as it stands. The short compact dream of this type is often most difficult to analyse and when it yields to analysis is often the most fruitful. This particular dream led to the most deep-seated phantasies of the dreamer's infantile fears of the inside of the mother's body. These latent thoughts were only accessible through associative material that was available when he thought of women who had characteristics the exact opposite of the woman in the dream.

Having stated the general rule I would now draw your attention to exceptions. There are dreams in which it is possible to read the meaning without the latent content, dreams of a simple type in which the symbolism is straightforward and typical. The dream I quoted in the first chapter in which the dreamer saw music in pictures which passed before her eyes, pictures of mountains and hills softly rounded, is an example. This dream could be evaluated at once, since it was the dream of a patient who had passed through a severe trauma, who was keeping contact with reality but struggling and finding it almost unbearable. The external reality situation of extreme frustration is compensated for by dreams of fulfilment of desire. Here is another dream that can be partly interpreted without latent content. A patient brought me at close intervals *dreams of being wheeled in a perambulator*. This patient was finding the effort to keep in touch with reality almost impossible. A young girl I had some time ago who had had a nervous breakdown brought me *dreams* for some weeks *in which everything had stopped.* Trains, buses, lifts, everything that in reality is only of value if it moves, had in her dreams come to a standstill. These dreams were important in their latent content, but I am illustrating here the fact that the manifest content as a whole can at times convey a meaning to the analyst. Dreams of making circumstances fit our physical requirements in order to prevent disturbance of sleep can be understood from manifest content. Here are some examples:

" *I dreamt I got out of bed to urinate.*" " *I dreamt I arrived in time for my early appointment.*" *I dreamt someone picked up the eiderdown from the floor and replaced it on my bed.*" Such dreams yield up an immediate significance.

I pass next to another type of evaluation to be gained from dreams.

These are dreams in which the latent content may be of significance, but not of such importance as the psychological purpose which the whole dream fulfils. The manifest content of the dream will not necessarily give the purpose of the dream as in the case of the examples I have cited. The dream will yield up its latent meaning through analysis, and yet to direct the analysis to ascertaining the meaning of the different elements is to miss the chief significance of the dream as a whole. Dreams sometimes serve as a means of placating the analyst, and so assuaging anxiety about the phantasies that have been transferred to the analyst. In this situation it is not the analysis of the actual dream that is important, but the analysis of the necessity to placate. A male patient, for example, who is dealing with unconscious aggressive phantasies towards the father figure, and therefore is unconsciously fearful of the analyst's attack, will often produce numbers of dreams which have the total significance of placation. They are a gift to turn away the imagined wrath of the avenger.

In another type of dream one must think of purpose rather than of latent content, namely when a long dream requires half an hour to recount, or a series of dreams take up the same length of time. Content may be important, but of first importance is the finding out of the unconscious purpose that is being served by the occupation of half an hour in recounting the dreams. I have known ten dreams to be recorded by one patient in this way. Among the purposes thus served I have found: (*a*) Resistance to speaking of present-day occurrences. (*b*) The dreams may represent potency, urethral, anal and sexual. (*c*) They may be symbolic gifts. (*d*) They may represent a gift following a withholding. When dreams are written out and read by the patient I often find they represent a good fæcal product, which in contrast to a childhood accident is given neatly and confined to the paper.

I remember an occasion upon which a patient said after recounting a number of dreams, " I am remembering a poem by Yeats, in which he says:

I, being poor, have only my dreams;
Tread softly, for you tread on my dreams.

The significance of the dreams was thus immediately clear. They were a love gift to the analyst. Their significance is still more detailed, for the inference is that the dreams are on the floor, and must be trodden on very softly. The child's mess on the floor may as easily mean a gift as an assault, " Tread softly, for you tread on my dreams."

I have spoken of the dream as a whole serving the purpose of placating, but sometimes the actual manifest content will do this. For example, the manifest content will sometimes give in direct form a phantasy that carries on some interpretation the analyst has given the day before. The dream betrays this by the completeness of its confirmation. An astute patient of my own generally recognizes this and says frankly " This dream is to oblige." The " obliging dream " is a placating one. It resembles the obedience of a fearful child. The analyst, when the patient is well versed in the main problems of psycho-analysis, must be on the alert when a dream presents a perfect " complex." The safeguard here lies in the analysis of the associations and the affects of the patient.

On the other hand we have in contrast to the patient who will obligingly tell us we are right and go on and confirm our interpretations the one who must prove we are wrong, and who will follow up an interpretation we have given by a dream which will prove us wrong. In both these types of dreams the analysis must be directed to the purpose of the dream rather than the content.

Another evaluation concerning dreams may be made from the patient's own attitude to them. Not only do patients differ in their attitudes to their own dreams but the same patient will have different attitudes at varying times. Some tend to undervalue dreams and others do the reverse. One finds on the whole that patients who have the greatest difficulty in bringing into the analysis their present-day emotions as they experience them with regard to people and affairs, who in reality find it difficult to express their opinions and criticisms inside and outside analysis, use their dreams as a means of diverting the attention and interest of the analyst from the patient's daily life. One may know much about unconscious phantasies, much of the patient's childhood, and yet fail to see the interrelation between these and the present-day conflicts. Such patients are often distressed if there are no dreams to recount and even feel they are not progressing and cannot progress unless dreams are forthcoming. In such cases, important as the help is that dreams will give, the objective on the part of the analyst must be the present-day stimuli, reality situations present and past, and suppressed transference affects.

Of the opposite type is the patient who clings to reality and resists all attempts to penetrate into the phantasy life. Such patients frequently undervalue dream-material. One patient I know rationalizes even this fact by saying he welcomes dreams when he can get them because then he feels he is truly getting something direct from his unconscious. In his case this means: " My unconscious has pro-duced this and therefore I am not responsible."

In two situations I have learned to surmise an important dream is being held back though it is not invariably so. In anxiety cases where a certain amount of analysis has been done, or in cases where anxiety has been released, I correlate an excessive outburst of anxiety with the following probable conditions:

(*a*) a present-day stimulus is not remembered during the analytical hour.

(*b*) a repressed event or phantasy that this stimulus has activated is near to consciousness.

(*c*) a dream of the night before has been forgotten or delayed in the telling.

Again with patients who are intellectualists and whose affects are difficult to release I find very often that an hour that has been baffling in that the patient does not seem to be able to do more than switch from one topic to another has ended with a recall of the dream of the previous night. In such cases I find that on the following day the analysis of this dream can proceed and one gets some light on the reason why the dream was delayed in the telling. Sometimes this may be because of latent content; at others the significance will lie in the transference situation and the fact of retention.

One may have the experience of a baffling analytical hour and then be told the following day by the patient that he remembered a dream after he had gone away. Such delayed dreams are mainly important because of latent content and worth subsequent inquiry.

A common resistance dream is one in which the patient dreams that he is telling the analyst something of great importance. It is " only a dream " and that is itself the reassurance. The matter of great importance need not be hoped for on that day. I remember a very marked instance of this type of dream in my experience with a patient who had an actual repressed traumatic sexual experience at the age of four. Before we really began to get indications of this fact she had many dreams of a young girl with a great secret which caused her sorrow and she, the patient, in the dream would plead with this girl to give her her confidence and reveal what the secret trouble was. The girl would remain obdurate. These dreams were most distressing in affect and baffling in analysis and yet they were most revealing in the sense that one was ultimately led to the revelation of an actual trauma.

I will only refer to typical dreams very briefly. A " crowd " in a dream indicates a secret. The analyst's work is to find the secret. Examination and train dreams however typical will have their individual nuances. Train dreams are used for many purposes. I gave one in the second lecture illustrating oral and anal phantasies. Such dreams will at times be accompanied by anxiety, where they are expressing past situations of incontinence of urine, as for example when the dreamer cannot catch the train since he arrives too late. The analyst's task is to discover a present-day emotional situation comparable to a past one in which the physical accompaniment was incontinence of urine. " Train " dreams can express indecision concerning some problem, as for example when the dreamer is actually in time for the train and then at last fails to board it. The analyst has the task of finding out what this symbolized " doubt " really means.

I should like to call your attention to the type of dream that symbolizes bodily functioning and bodily sensations.

In an earlier chapter I said that intuitive knowledge is experienced knowledge, and that the unconscious is a storehouse of experience which we may have forgotten but have never lost. The experiences of the body ego from earliest infancy can be found in dreams if we can understand them. Dreams will sometimes present us with evidence of bodily experiences before the child was articulate and others will give us knowledge of present-day suppressed experiences. An example of a simple dream that gave evidence of present-day suppressed bodily experience is: "*I dreamt I was picking flowers last night.*" We can infer from this that masturbation occurred the night of the dream.

A dream of distress concerning the hearing of a mighty wind will often be stimulated by actual flatulence. Such dreams are of frequent occurrence. There are dreams of this type that give us bodily experiences of very early years and no actual memory will ever be forthcoming, but the body remembers and the eye once having seen has stored a picture which a dream can reproduce. For example, "*I was running one way on one side of the railings and a man in shorts was running the opposite way on the other side of the railings.*" "I was running" in the dream proved during analysis to be a pictorial representation of bodily experience of urinating. The "opposite way" referred to the observation of her father's "running" which was different from hers. The "railings" were the intervening bars of the cot bed.

Here is another example. A patient described quite vividly a special place on a road, this road being an element in his dream. He knew exactly how many yards he was from this object and that object. Then he said: "But if I can say so accurately just where I was I must have been quite stationary.

86

The place was stationary and yet I told you I was moving." From the content of the hour the interpretation of "stationary and yet moving" was that he was urinating.

I find that on to all kinds of machinery and movable apparatus can be transferred bodily sensations, especially those experienced at an early age. These are a few examples: " *I was in a room and suddenly the door opened and a great flood of water came in.*" This is interesting enough as the evidence of an " accident," but it is the one dream that I am bold enough to quote as possibly embodying also a birth experience. It was ascertained that the patient's birth was heralded by an unexpected sudden bursting of the waters. The fact was unknown to the patient at the time of the dream. " *I was in a lift and suddenly it went down flop.*" This dream I found to be the representation of an experience of fluid excreta rushing down and flopping on the floor. Here is an assurance in a dream dealing with the same anxiety experience in childhood. The dreamer said: " *I saw a marvellous thing happen. A ' car ' went straight up a building on the outside somehow and got safely to a garage, I suppose on the upper storey.*" The associations to this dream through references made to the way in which a dentist's chair works up and down brought the memory of the patient's baby's chair that could be made higher and lower. The dreamer had no actual memory of herself in the chair, but the dream undoubtedly dramatized an experience where instead of the " car " (Ka Ka) going up safely into a garage it came down much to the anxiety of the little child. The dream had further significances.

On to the mechanism of the chair were transferred the bodily sensations felt while the child was in the chair, and from this dream the inference could be made that the accident occurred in the chair. To another patient I am indebted for this very valuable dream. The patient dreamt he was trying to get rid of fæces in a lavatory pan, and then it filled up with water instead of emptying. The phantasies involved in this dream were of importance, but I think even then their full significance can only be realized by the understanding of an actual happening. Here in this dream we have a representation of what it felt like first to try to pass a motion and then the subsequent experience of an enema administration.

Here is another dream of the same type. *The dreamer thought he was in a passage with a mop which he was using to swab it out.* During the hour's analysis the patient recounted a conversation of the evening before when someone had said: "Your ears are not set quite alike." After telling me this, the patient covered his ears with his hands. The dream stimulated the patient to give phantasies and associations that had reference both to fæcal matter and hair. The gesture of covering the ears had the significance of both preventing his own hearing and being heard, protecting himself and protecting me. But to understand more fully the significance of the ears and particular inhibitions in connection with hearing and the over-determination of phantasy about ears, other facts have to be taken into account. The patient had an operation on his ear too early for him to retain any conscious memory of it. Underlying all phantasy there is in this dream an inherent body-memory as well: the passage was

88

actually an ear passage that was once swabbed out. In this dream the man is the active doer, not the passive agent. A stimulus for the dream in addition to the reference to ears in the conversation of the evening before was that for a few seconds during his analysis of the previous day the maid was dusting the stairs outside the consulting room. I registered this fact but it was noticeable that the patient made no reference to this at the time.

In the interpretation of dreams the analyst can turn to account the gestures or minor actions performed by the patient during the analytic hour. The technique in this way approximates in adult analysis to the principles of play-technique with children. One has to interpret actions or gestures as either dramatizing the dream in some symbolic way or as a means of dealing with anxiety by correcting the impulse or event in the dream. Here are some illustrations of these different purposes of actual dramatization during analysis.

The patient who dreamt of the eiderdown slipping off the bed and of its being put over her again, suddenly felt cold during the analysis and put her coat over her. The dream gives first an experience of the night before when she really was cold and did not wish to wake up to adjust the eiderdown, and so dreamt it was done for her. This was a convenience dream. The repetition of the situation during the analytical hour, however, needed inquiry, for the room was warm.

Here is an example of dramatization during analysis that must be interpreted alongside the dream material. The purpose served by the dramatization was that the anxiety inherent in the dream was resolved, for the actions were the exact opposite of the repressed memory and wish. The patient, a man, came in and lay down on the couch. A second afterwards he thrust his hands in his pocket. " Hullo," he said, in great surprise. " What's this ? " He drew out a crumpled envelope, looked at it and then said: "Oh, it's nothing, waste paper that's all." He then went on talking in the usual way. A little later he thrust his hand in his pocket again and suddenly got up saying: " I can't stand this any longer, where's your wastepaper basket ? I must get this into the wastepaper basket." Still later in the hour when talking about a MS. he was at work upon he said: " Look here, I must just see if I made those corrections," and he jumped up again and went to his attaché case, looked at his MS., and came back with a sigh of relief, " Yes, it's all right, I corrected the errors."

His dream was: " *There were two visitors and I was bothered as to where they would sleep. I put one of them in a bed I knew was to spare. I gave the other visitor my bed, but then I had nowhere to sleep myself.*"

The relevant associations during the hour taken in conjunction with the actions I have recorded proved that we were dealing with a repressed incident in early life when the rubbish was not deposited in the wastepaper basket, since it occurred at an early age when he could not correct his errors and as a consequence his parents were turned out of their bed because of the small visitor.

Conversation dreams often prove difficult of analysis. I have learned to recognize the following types. The persons conversing will often represent different aspects of the dreamer's psyche under the guise of different people. In some dreams the conversation will contain words or phrases that have been incorporated because of their own significance or because of the importance of the person who uttered them. Sometimes such an incorporated phrase of the present day may overlay a phrase used by someone in the patient's past. In the " cockatoo " dream I quoted in the last lecture one has an example of two people conversing who represent different parts of the psyche, while the word " cockatoo " itself was an element worth investigating on its own account.

Dreams containing numbers are often difficult to analyse and they do not always repay the inquiry. If one can evoke from the patient something concrete associated with the specific number, it will often lead to a valuable interpretation. One must always remember the term " figure " means shape as well as number. One patient of mine has always maintained that " four " is a feminine number. We have had many symbolical interpretations of the number four which are easy to supply. I never felt convinced about the significance of " four " in this instance until the patient recalled a bedroom scene and said: " You know I remember watching my mother undress when I was a tiny boy. She always plaited her hair in four long tails." " Four " thus became a feminine number for him and the satisfaction in the fact was that the tails were an assurance of masculinity. The number five often ultimately refers to the five fingers and hence to infantile masturbation. A man dreamt that *a husband and wife were together for five days*. The subtle nuance of this dream was to be found through a reference he made to the book of Genesis. He recalled that it was on the sixth day that God made man and on the seventh day he called his whole creation very good. In the dream husband and wife were together five days only.

A patient of mine had an appointment for the first time at the Clinic. He did not arrive at the appointed time, for he tried to find the clinic at number "sixty-three." A dream revealed that "sixty-three" was the number of a house in a certain district where he had once been told prostitutes were to be found.

A dream of the number 180 was interpreted for me during an analytical session as meaning "I ate nothing."

Colours in dreams are very important for one of my patients. I always ask for more details concerning any colour, and in addition, if the colour is pertaining to material, I ask for details concerning the type of material. I have proved conclusively through this patient my surmise that both creative imagination and artistic appreciation are firmly rooted in the earliest reality experiences of taste, touch and sound. For this patient an oatmeal-coloured material had a "crunchy" feeling and the "crunchy" feeling in her fingers always brought sensation in her teeth.

A cherry coloured silk will make her mouth water and she longs to put her cheeks gently on its surface. The range of colours for this patient are in terms of cream, butter, lemon, orange, cherry, peach, damson, wine, plum, nut brown, chestnut brown. Materials can be crunchy like biscuits, soft like beaten white of eggs, thick like cake. Threads can be coarse like the grain of wholemeal bread, shine like the skin of satin. I do not let any reference to colour or material or to dress escape me in the dreams this patient brings.

Another interesting mechanism one patient unconsciously employs made it possible for me to deduce from a dream what reality situation stimulated it. The mechanism throws a light upon the complicated problem of the different methods by which stability of the psyche is achieved, a problem I believe of such immense complexity that we know little of it. We realize only the grosser mechanisms and nothing of the wheels within wheels that work together in the unity of a psyche more subtly than all the physiological forces that work together in the bodily organism. With this patient I only get a really definite dream of hostility to mother, father, brothers and sisters in certain conditions. Many dreams have shown veiled hostile wishes, but a plain uncamouflaged dream of hostility, of actual death wishes, is forthcoming only if in reality there has been the direct stimulus of hearing actual appreciation of the person who afterwards figures in the dream as the object of hostile wishes. If the patient hears unexpectedly words of praise concerning any relative she dreams of that relative in a hostile manner. So marked has this been that I can guess the reality stimulus of an open hostile dream. The explanation is not as simple as it appears It is only to be understood by appreciating the problem of how and in what manner the psyche maintains its equilibrium of forces. Some people attain this by a much greater interplay with actual people in their environment; their lives so to speak are more psychically interwoven and played out with other people.

The patient of whom I speak had a fairly stable environment until the age of five and no external difficulty of a major type within that period. This meant a degree of genital development. An actual rival to the mother came into the household when the patient was five. This rival who won the father's affection was openly hostile to the mother. The consequence of this was a profound repression of the Œdipus situation in the patient. The hostile feelings to the mother were intolerable. They were embodied by one who was a real obstacle to the mother's happiness and not a phantasied one. The lasting influence of this real situation is given in the special mechanism by which dreams that express the original hostility felt towards her mother and the other children can be expressed. When someone real in the present-day environment is spontaneously appreciative of them then there comes a relaxation within the patient's psyche. We reach then in such dreams the original hostility felt before the trauma at the age of five years. This is the goal of the analysis in order that there may ensue attainment of an inner equilibrium rather than one that is dependent upon the environment. The importance of the time-factor in analysis is brought home to us since in a mechanism of this type the patient's contacts with reality, the dramatizations of the psychic life in these real situations have all to be explored with infinite patience.

I will summarize briefly the different evaluations of dreams.

Dream interpretation is a corner-stone of psycho-analytic technique. The analyst can gauge by dreams how closely he is keeping in touch with the patient's unconscious problem. They help him to understand the transference affects in terms of those same problems.

Dreams are a means of exploring present-day stimuli and current conflicts through the elaboration of pre-conscious thoughts. To understand the unity of psychical life, the interrelation of the pre-conscious with the unconscious must be known.

The latent content of the dream is arrived at by the method of free association to the different elements of the dream. This is dream analysis.

Dreams may prove of value apart from or in addition to the significance of the latent content. They may be used as a means of unconsciously placating the analyst, as symbolic of power, of control over fæcal product, as proof of control over the analyst. The dream may represent a love gift.

The patient's over-valuation or under-estimation of dreams is itself an aid to understanding the psychical problem.

Dreams often reveal both present-day bodily experiences and forgotten ones of childhood. The correlation of such bodily sensations with phantasy is the object of the analyst.

Characteristic gesture and behaviour needs to be correlated with the patient's associations in arriving at the meaning of a dream.

The interpretation of gesture and characteristic actions approximates to the play-technique in the analysis of children.

The key to the dramatization in real life of a major repressed traumatic situation may often be found through a dream.

The clue to the significance of conversation, numbers and colours in dreams can often be reached through the patient's associations to some specific person or specific object.

CHAPTER IV

Illustrations of Different Types of Dreams

1. Dream related by a "normal" young woman with strong ego-resistances.
2. Dream related by a man experiencing anxiety with regard to women.
3. Dream revealing the Œdipus situation in oral imagery.
4. Dream revealing a typical jealousy situation of childhood related by a woman of fifty.
5. Dream revealing phantasies displaced on to multiplication and genealogical tables.

THIS chapter will be devoted to a series of different types of dreams from the analyses of different patients. In connection with each I shall point out the material that was of importance in the progress of the analysis. This will be more in the nature of a résumé of the hour's work in each case and not an exhaustive examination of the whole material. I am not selecting analytical sessions which every analyst experiences when the patient's dreams and associations fit together like a classic on psycho-analysis and interpretation is easy to make. I shall give only one such example.

In this series of dreams the things of importance will be selected from a mass of material as in the last two lectures but in greater detail.

All dreams I give are of recent date because only so can one communicate a feeling of freshness and aliveness which contact with the living psyche should give. The present-day situation, the stimulus of the dream, the part played by the analyst, will be indicated as well as the main interpretations given.

Here is the first example. The patient dreamt *" she was going abroad and had reached Folkestone, only farther than Folkestone is in reality. Arrived there she found she had left her money, passport and ticket at home and she must go back home to fetch them. She thought she was going to Holland. She went back home and there was no one there but the charwoman, her father and mother were away. She found her belongings in her drawers quite safely, and it seemed all the more annoying to find them there, quite neatly and inevitably."*

In order to appreciate the actual analysis of this dream as far as it went in one hour the analyst's problem with regard to the patient must also be appreciated. Some interpretation of this dream could be made by a knowledge of symbols. I mean the *analyst* could do this, but that is not analysis of the patient. This patient is from a clinical point of view normal. Her phantasy life is under strong repression; she is immensely occupied by reality. " Free association " means for her a recounting of all that has happened in reality, but her private thinking and feeling is her own possession, and if I am to know it I must bide her time. The picture on the whole is of a person able to deal effectively with the external world. She is well endowed with humour and it is her greatest bulwark against anxiety. Along with repression of phantasy there is an inaccessibility of childhood memories. There is also a curious type of repression. For example, one can surmise from recurrence of certain types of dreams that some definite experience must have occurred and been forgotten. To such inference the patient listens and makes no response. Then suddenly on some subsequent day she will make a seemingly casual reference to the actual occurrence the dreams and associations have indicated and she will speak of the event as if it had always been in consciousness.

I want you to think of this dream not as an isolated one to be interpreted symbolically, but as one to be understood in terms of the particular difficulties this patient presents. I wish also to emphasize the principle that the latent thoughts and not the manifest content must concern us first.

The analysis previous to this dream had been occupied almost entirely by expressions of mild anger succeeded by some misery due to the fact that an expected letter had not arrived. It was a week overdue. I select from the previous hour in the light of the dream-hour's analysis one sentence out of all the references she made to the man who disappointed her by the delayed letter. " All my other friends," she said, " do all they can to please *me*; he is the one whom *I* most wish to please, would most desire to please." The patient had also during the previous week-end visited a friend, but the night had been spent in a house where the people were strangers. It was noticeable in her anxiety about the letter that greatly anticipated as this week-end had been, no reference was made to it.

At the close of the first hour I could do no more than say that she had a real situation at the moment that was occupying her attention and that I thought we should find some of her unhappiness was accentuated by unknown misery and anxiety belonging to other situations that could be linked on or could lie behind the present one, and at the moment these situations were inaccessible.

The following day was the day after the dream. She informed me immediately that she had had the delayed letter and was happy again. Out of the hour's material I select the patient's following remarks as being most pertinent to the analytical problem. (*a*) The flowers in that vase of yours are lovely. The flowers in the other are not as good, the colour of the vase isn't right; it's the wrong brown, but the others are lovely. (*b*) I'm longing to get on with my jumper. I'd like it finished at once. I've a new stitch to do. I want to see how the jumper looks when it's made. The trouble is about wool. Strange how shops don't stock the right brown, the brown I want. You see the wool in made-up things—in jumpers already knitted—but one can't get the actual colour in wool and make it one's self. I want wool like the dark brown of your cushion." (*c*) The woman who takes my old clothes has written to me it's all right, she'll take them, but how absurd never to tell me she was going to have a baby. That's why I have not heard from her. At this point the patient told the dream. She continued: (*d*) " I can't think why Holland, but I am sure I have a feeling that the name Holland was lying about somewhere."

Then I interposed at once, saying " How do you *feel* a *name* lying about ? " To this she replied: " Well, that brings to my mind the Holland smocks I wore when I was a child, some were coloured and spots were embroidered on them, but I remember nothing else about them. Neither can I think why

Folkestone. I feel sure I went there with my nurse, Had she a sister living there? I can't think where I went from. There seemed to be white cliffs in the dream, so very white. But I can only think of Dover. A bleak place Dover is to land at when you feel horrid after the crossing and you've been ghastly sick. But Dover reminds me of Dieppe and going there with father, and it was great fun. We had so little time to catch the bus to where we were going and I managed the customs slickly and got the luggage taken away and on to the bus in no time, and he was so very pleased with me. I never told you about the week-end. You know I so often leave things behind me. I thought I would be careful this time, especially as my hosts were strangers. I felt sure I had packed everything and I was going down the path when I remembered I'd left something in the bedroom. I didn't want to be laughed at, the door was open, so I crept upstairs and got my belongings and crept out again and no one ever knew; it was splendid. I did not want them to know! "

I will now give you the interpretations I made to the patient during the hour. I linked her remark about her father's pleasure with her desire expressed the day before to please the man from whom she awaited the letter. I said: " X belongs to the class of men to whom you want to be pleasing, descended from, of the same lineage as your father." She said: " Oh yes, I see what you mean." I said: " You must feel towards X as you once felt towards your father." I pointed out that in her reference to Dieppe she had pleased her father by her prompt-ness in getting things in, in being in time, by catching

the bus. I referred to her finding her things in
" drawers " all neat and tidy. Her anxiety at not
receiving her letter had made her think that she
was not pleasing X. She had thoughts that X might
be finding someone more pleasing than herself,
and most important of all that her letters were not
entertaining to him. These two trains of thought
suggested moreover the opposite possibility, namely
that her father would be displeased at an inability
to get things out of the way, at luggage left about
and that X might dislike what she wrote to him.

I referred to the leaving of her belongings about
at the week-end, the creeping back again and out
lest she should be heard and be laughed at. I
referred to the dream and her finding her father
and mother out and only the charwoman there.
" But," I said, " she wouldn't matter, as it's her
business to clean up, isn't it ? Yet, having got back
to where there was only the charwoman, it was all
right in another way. You found your things in
your ' drawers.' Your anxiety was still further
allayed, but your annoyance was now felt because
everything was neat and tidy. I linked this with
her state of mind of the day before. She had felt
miserable for nothing, the letter was awaiting her
at home. There was a feeling of anti-climax, a
great pother that had arisen in her mind that
needed a *real* grievance, and she felt in a way
thwarted when she found the letter. She was
happy in having the letter in reality, but the feeling
of anti-climax remained and this I said had nothing
to do with the letter itself but with unconscious
memories and anxieties that had been stirred by the
delay of the letter.

I said that her father was the important person in a forgotten incident. The man had to be pleased, she felt anxiety lest she should not please him, and from this I inferred not only a love attitude to him but an anger against him for reasons not yet plain, which made the desire to please over-accentuated, to make up for something we might call " fear " of him. She wanted her letter from X yesterday terribly. When a child wants something terribly and can't get it, then anger is aroused and the desire to get what it wants is fused with hate and thus breeds fear of the one who withholds.

I referred to her wanting the brown wool and her impatience of the shop attendant who could not produce what she wanted. I said, " You see the wool you want for your work in jumpers that are already made. It is to be had, people do have it and yet it is inaccessible to you. You want to make something, you want to have what others can have. I have cushions of the colour you want."

I now referred to the new baby she had mentioned. Then I gathered together the references that indicated an unconscious phantasy concerning the making of babies, the brown wool for jumpers, the putting of things together neatly, and I contrasted this with references to things that represent untidiness, such as the luggage strewn over the platform, the seasickness, the old clothes. I referred to the embroidered spots on her Holland overall as a cover memory for dirty marks. I contrasted via her dream, the white cliffs of Dover and the seasickness after a voyage. I reminded her of the phrase " I can't think where I went from." I said this phrase was very significant, the hint it gave of an actual episode of dirtying herself, and of doing it at a time of stress and anxiety consequent upon separation from her parents. I said we could not be sure whether we had got the actual facts regarding details of place and time, but that we had reached an event of psychological importance when her anxiety and anger was shown by a sudden evacuation of the bowels. Her parents were not there, and I believed her phantasy when she was sent away to Folkestone with her nurse was that her mother and father were making a baby. Again the phrase " I can't think where I went from " I interpreted as covering the thought " Where did I come from," that is, from what place in the mother do babies come ? I surmised this phantasy by her remark about the woman who took her old clothes. " If she had told me she was having a baby I would not have bothered her." The inference I drew was that the bother indicated by the dream was that she thought her mother was making a baby. I said there was at the time she went to Folkestone a desire to make a baby herself, to make it in the way she could phantasy, that is, by a solid stool, and that she had contrasted the liquid fæces with the solid stool and that liquid fæces meant anger and mess, but solid fæces that could be safe even in the " drawers," meant being pleasing and represented a love gift, an echo of which we heard in her pleasure that her father approved of the way she dealt with the luggage.

I will now make an estimation of this hour's work. (a) We have gained historically by evidence of a stressful time when the child dirtied herself by a sudden evacuation and that it occurred when she was separated from her parents.

We have direct evidence of where the present-day father fixation lies, that the attitude to the father imago is one of ambivalence, anxiety due to repressed anger making it imperative for her to be assured she is pleasing to him. This is the most important revelation this hour gives as far as estimating where and how this patient can gain from analysis. Unless this attitude is modified it will blind her to one most important factor for happiness. Occupied by her desire to be pleasing to a man who is a father imago she will not estimate in reality how much or how little the real man is pleasing to *her*.

We have in this hour gained access to the anal and oral phantasies of birth as well as indications of anger expressed anally.

We have also seen that the reactions of tidiness and control have been largely influenced by love and fear of the father. Implied in this though not explicit we may expect to find that the anger against the mother, envy and hostility towards her is under the control of the influence of the love and fear of the father.

The mother transference within the analysis is shown by reference to the brown colour of the cushion which she wants for herself and to the flowers in the vases, approved and disapproved, these being the vehicles of her phantasies concerning her wish for babies. An interesting corroboration of the interpretation of this dream occurred the following week-end. After it, on Monday, I was told the following. ' She had arranged for a pleasant afternoon on the previous Saturday to be spent on the river with a girl friend. She found on meeting her friend that the latter had arranged something quite different and the new plan included a motor trip to Folkestone. The patient said: "And all done without consulting me ! I am expected to fall in with her arrangements and she says nothing about my disappointment. I know ' K ' doesn't intend to make me feel a child, an unpractical person who can't look after herself, but it's absurd how she does make me think that that is how she feels about me. I'm glad I had the guts to say I would not go to Folkestone."

From this coincidence of a suggested present-day visit to Folkestone we can estimate the strength of the emotional stress felt when she was a child, sent to Folkestone with her nurse while her parents were away together. On this occasion she can refuse to go and she can express her anger and disappointment in words. "And all done without consulting me."

The next dream I select was told by a male patient. This man is strongly fixated to his mother. I do not think this statement conveys much. Many men are mother-fixated, but that does not make mother-fixated men all alike. The situation can be appreciated more if I tell you he was an only child upon whom the mother devoted her whole attention and that the mother was a more dominating figure than the father. The psychological environment she provided played upon every natural anxiety a child is prone to by virtue of its elemental impulses. She was often ill. The child indulged in no ordinary childish escapade without being told that such behaviour made his mother ill. Every infantile omnipotent belief in the power to harm and destroy the being whom he first loved, then hated and feared because of frustration, was reinforced by the external environment. Both mother and father curtailed his play because of the effect he was told it would have either upon his mother or upon himself.

I have deduced during the course of the analysis that one traumatic moment not explicitly remembered in this patient's childhood was the observation of menstrual blood. I have not yet been able to fix an appropriate date, but the importance of that observation and the apprehension aroused by it is to be estimated in conjunction with the fact that his mother told him in childhood that his first tooth came before he was weaned and she had to wean him because he hurt her breast.

The main problem in this analysis is the terror of the woman's body. His rooted unconscious belief is that he is responsible for what to him is a mutilated body and the analysis pursues a tortuous course in bringing to light the ways with which he combats this belief.

The dream to which I will give the patient's chief associations ran: " *I saw a lady who had black stuff round the top of her body covering the breasts and black stuff round her hips hiding her genitals, only the middle part of her body was naked.*"

Having in his usual way dispensed with the dream by relating it, and having dispensed with the week-end by telling me the places he had visited, the patient turned with relief (having given me an anal gift), to something that really interested him. The story took nearly half an hour to relate. It concerned some physiological illustrations that had been drawn by a medical colleague for the purpose of making slides for a lantern. They were first drawn on a huge scale on very large sheets of paper, in great detail and coloured red. These had to be reduced in scale for the purpose of lantern slides. The patient went into great details that I cannot repeat because I did not understand the technicalities. When the slides were eventually shown the colour was wrong. Then the patient laughed and said " only if it had been possible to use a black light would those diagrams have shown red on the sheet."

The story with all its scientific technicalities took nearly half an hour to tell and before it was ended I was debating as to how I could evoke more relevant material. But once again, as so often is my experience, I was glad I let the patient get to his problem along his own path. Directly he said " a black light would have thrown up the colour red," I said: " That is the meaning of the black in the dream, isn't it ? From black we can infer red." His immediate reply was: " It can be what bloody colour you like." Incidentally this is a neat example of the " return of the repressed." Having thus expressed himself he dispensed once more with the subject he was relating and started afresh. This time it was a shorter story of a person who had been ill and who had been to a nursing home. He finished this account by the remark: " A nursing home is a cover for a multitude of sins." Here again I interpolated. " The black was a cover in the dream, wasn't it ?—genitals and breasts as nursing homes." Again he rejoined " bloody."

Once more he endeavoured to get away from the topic. He remembered the week-end and now with a considerable emotion of anger he told me he had been at work upon a pit that was being dug out in order that an open-air bath might be constructed. He had worked upon this all the morning and devised an outlet for water; much time and energy had been spent on the work. After he had had lunch he went back to resume the work and found that two girls had interfered with the water channel and silted it up again. The patient was silent a moment and then he uttered fiercely: " Bloody."

The affect passed quite quickly and in a matter-of-fact tone he began again. " A girl I know suffers from corns. I gave her some corn cure and I told her how to apply it. I told her to be very careful when she pulled it off. If she wasn't careful she would leave the skin red and raw and inflamed."

I think this analytical excerpt gives a characteristic hour's work when one is dealing with an anxiety situation, the ramifications of which are not yet explored. The transference situation is clear enough. The analyst is the figure in the dream, the substitute mother-imago. The patient could do little more by way of expressing his anxiety and terror of me than hurl the word " bloody " at me.

The period of the onset of this anxiety in his own life, with which he is now dealing can be estimated by reference to the huge detailed drawings. Just so enormous was the mother to the tiny child, just so enormous in the phantasy operating at the moment in the analysis is the analyst. The expletive is symbolical of the thing ejected at the being of whom he was and is afraid. The red nipple, the red genitals fuse with the repressed memory of seeing menstrual blood. One surmises that the black also refers to the pubic hair of the mother's genitals, and that the " red and raw under black " is associated also with some early sight of a little girl's genitals.

His fury at having his water channel interfered with carried over his anxiety concerning the projected, expected intention to harm his own penis as a reprisal arising from his belief that he is responsible for mutilation, a phantasied mutilation first associated with the breasts and later the genitals.

Finally the theme appears in connection with the incident of the corns; the taking out of the corns is an alleviation of pain and thus the perfect obverse of the underlying phantasy. The solicitude and careful instructions given to the girl in order that the skin might not be raw and inflamed tells us clearly, along with all the other associations, that his belief was that in his phantasy his mother had been castrated.

An important thing to realize in connection with the released anxiety is the fact that he had been able to engage in the type of manual pursuit that would have caused anxiety to his own mother. He laboured arduously and got very hot, one thing forbidden him as child and boy. Any work or play that made him perspire was forbidden because of his mother's fear that he might catch cold. A considerable gain therefore has been achieved. To this must be added the symbolical importance of the actual task he was engaged upon, namely the digging out of the sand from the pit. His mother's reactions to dirt were such that he was terrified of getting his clothes dirty. His own unconscious fears concerning his aggressive anal phantasies and the primitive wish to get the fæcal power whatever that represented such as food, children, his father's penis from inside her were accentuated by his mother's reactions. Thus his ability to indulge in digging out the sand tells us of the lessening of fears with regard to this phantasy; the digging and the sand have become more symbolical, less actually the mother's body. Something is being done in the analysis to bring to conscious realization the aggressive wishes by the establishment of links between the id and consciousness via the preconscious mind. It is this process that will finally enable him to believe both that he had and has aggressive wishes and secondly that they were and are not omnipotent. His wishes did not in reality injure his mother's genitals nor did he take from her all her other babies. He was an only child, a fact re-enforcing the unconscious phantasy.

Eight or nine years ago an American girl was three years in analysis with me. She came to me after visiting a number of doctors, among them eminent neurologists. She had undergone rest cures and occupation therapy. Her major neurotic breakdown occurred in early womanhood. When abroad she was given sedative drugs and the practice carried on after her return home. When she came for analytic treatment, and for months afterwards, she could not venture out until after dark and then never alone. She was suffering at that time from severe depression. Early environmental factors were not conducive to mental health. She was the daughter of a medical officer in residence at an asylum and as a tiny child she was taken by her father regularly on his rounds through the wards. There were serious disagreements between her parents. Her mother went away for long holidays during her early childhood. Thanks to an admirable and warm-hearted nurse the little girl had one stable person in her childhood.

The analysis was very incomplete, but the depressions passed, the fears of going out left her, and anxieties were alleviated. The patient married.

The patient sought my help again after an interval of eight years. She arrived in a very tearful state saying that she felt as she did as a child and as she did when she had analysis before. The actual trouble was that she was terrified because she wanted to keep on urinating. She was running to the lavatory every few minutes, and she was terrified of going out because of the need to urinate constantly. She cried all the time she was talking to me.

I learned the following facts: Her mother was on the point of returning home after a long sojourn abroad. Her sister who had been away for years had returned home a short time ago. She had brought with her a small daughter who had been born abroad. The following facts were given: the patient's favourite cat had had some ailment and instead of being clean he made water all over the house and had been " despatched." Further, she had a great shock one day on going into her husband's waiting room to see a patient sitting on a chair and making water quite placidly.

After these incidents had been related the patient

said she could recognize that the panic she was feeling about making water was the same panic she used to have when she was a child and was terrified lest she should wet her drawers. She would scream out: "Quick, Nannie, quick." Her drawers might not get unfastened in time.

From the first few hours of analysis during this second period of treatment while the patient was in great anxiety, I select the hour in which she related this dream: "*I was in a bedroom and a man was giving a woman some wine and I wanted some. He didn't give me any but he came over to my bed and kissed me.* I woke up feeling happier."

Associations to her sister came first to her mind. She remarked: "Although I did not want to see her at all it was strange when I was on the platform and actually saw her come out of the carriage I felt like breaking down and crying my eyes out. She had the little girl with her. Of course I had not seen her before."

The patient talked about her cat. She was grieved for what had happened, but she said " it was such a nuisance. I had to run about after it and wipe up after it. I had to leave whatever I was doing, and could not attend to anything but the cat. It occupied my whole attention." Then the patient spoke of how little attention her sister's child needed, but still she felt as if the whole family had descended on her. She would be glad when she and her husband were alone again with no one to interfere. Her mother had arrived and had called the previous evening. She had begun at once to make plans to take the patient and her husband to dinner parties, theatres and motor rides. " Of course," said the patient, "I became more and more agitated knowing that I couldn't go with her now that this anxiety about going to the lavatory possesses me. I was afraid to tell her about having treatment, thinking she would be cross and impatient with me that, after all this time, I was ill again as I had been before. I got so agitated that at last I burst into tears and she asked what was the matter. I told her all about it and I was quite astonished. I was amazed that she was kind and understanding. She gave me money straight away for treatment. I actually went with her on a bus to her hotel after that. Poor mother, I feel sorry for her. But that seems ridiculous with all this fuss about myself. Why, instead of being sorry for myself should I feel sorry for her ? She is well and independent and has a gay life. Why do I feel sorry for her and I want to say to her just as I did as a tiny child: ' Nannie, I'm sorry.' I suppose it was when I had ' accidents ' but I don't remember the accidents, all I remember is fear of them and calling ' Quick, Nannie.' It is awful to have to wait at a moment like that. To-day I ventured to do some shopping but I got into a panic waiting for the shop assistant to give me my purchase. He seemed so long I felt sure I should have to dash out to find a lavatory. I wanted to call out to him ' Be quick.' I told you about the cat and about the woman who made a mess in the waiting room, but I don't think I told you about our last holiday. I wonder if that was a stimulus too for this outbreak of anxiety. We had a bedroom with french windows opening on to a balcony. We kept the windows wide open. One night we woke to find a tremendous storm raging. After a time I thought we ought to close the windows and to my horror I found the room flooded with water and we couldn't get the windows closed. We had to wake up the proprietor and he made a frightful fuss. He said the carpets would be spoilt. The person in the room beneath ours ran upstairs. The water was dripping through the ceiling from our room into his. We had a dreadful time baling out the water and we thought we should have damages to pay, but next day things weren't so bad, in the night they were pretty hellish. Strange I haven't thought of this incident before."

Then she continued: " It suddenly came to me last night that I had always told you that I never remembered being in my parents' bed. All I remembered was wanting to go in and Nannie saying I was too big a girl. But I remember quite clearly now going to them in the mornings and being in bed with them. That's strange to think of, as strange as thinking my mother once fed me as a baby. I shouldn't think my sister will have more babies. You know my mother went away for quite long times when I was tiny. But I had Nannie and I think my father was very fond of me. I remember how I used to go about with him round the wards and round the garden."

This case is illuminating for several reasons. One of these is the fact that after an interval of eight years the analytic work proceeded where it left off, as if there had been no interval. The patient got immediate further insight. She realized the early setting of her panic in childhood as she had never done before and attached to it one of the right reasons. Moreover, memories not previously in consciousness came now with ease.

The next point of interest is to see how analysis immediately proceeded to a deeper level from the place where it terminated. In the hour I have reported I did nothing except summarize at the end of the hour. The spur of anxiety was releasing thoughts, memories and phantasies. Repressed anxiety did not cause circumlocutions. It is the patient's conviction, not the analyst's, that has dynamic value. In such hours one's care should be non-interference. One does not want to lose any phantasy, memory or affect that may be forthcoming.

The cardinal interpretations made were in connection with the aggressive phantasy of destroying by water. The rivalry with the mother for the father's wine was pointed out—correlated with the impatience with the shopkeeper for keeping her waiting. I was able to say: "Be quick, I'm going to urinate" was identical with her rage at not being given what she wanted when she was a baby, and that the dream indicated a time when she had transferred love from her mother to her father, and that her making water was a hostile act against her mother. I was able to show the patient that why she felt sorry for her mother was that omnipotently she thought she had brought about two results. (1) Her mother went away when she was quite little for long holidays, and later her mother and father became alienated. (2) Her mother had no more children after herself and this again unconsciously was the omnipotent fulfilment of her aggressive wishes.

I pass to another illustration of a very different kind. It is taken from the analysis of the woman of fifty to whom I have already referred. The dream I shall give occurred at the end of about four months of analysis. I have spoken of one neurotic manifestation, namely that she was unable to settle for long in any home and that for years her husband and she had lived in house after house to which she subsequently took a dislike. She had a querulous disposition and suffered at times from depression. She deplored these traits but had no power to control them. I said in reference to this case that it was possible in the first week of analysis for the analyst to know that one of her major problems was that unconsciously she believed herself responsible for the death of her small brother at the age of one and a half years when she herself was two and a half years old. The psychical fabric of her life for forty-seven years was inter-woven with this belief, and I indicated that though the analyst could have given this interpretation in the first week it would have been impossible for such an interpretation to have been accepted, or if accepted, it could only have been by lip-service. The patient was an ardent ritualist in religion. Everything that pertained to the physical life was obnoxious to her. She longed to go into retreat and to pursue spiritual practices. She had heard psycho-analysis " had to do with sex." If that were true she would not continue with it. She went to con-fession regularly and I gathered that she told her priest what transpired in analysis, but I never heard actually what she said to the priest or what the priest said to her. She had only six months to get what help she could from psycho-analysis because her husband was preparing still another home after a period of holiday and residence in an hotel.

What alleviation of her trouble could occur within six months clearly depended upon my wariness in avoiding becoming the bad parent in comparison with the holy father. She was constantly on the alert lest I should talk to her " about anything horrid." I do not think during the six months I was ever the first to speak of anything bearing on sexual problems. When I did so I followed her lead and went only a little farther than she did. I had a satisfactory result from that as far as it went. She had had no intimacy with her husband for many years. She had always been frigid when they had intercourse, but for years they had had separate beds and had kept apart. Towards the end of the analysis she confessed with great reluctance, shame, surprise and annoyance, that she crept one night into her husband's bed for him to caress her. She could not understand herself.

There was not an interpretation I gave this patient that was not subject to much consideration on my part, a surmise about the type of reaction her particular psyche as a whole was likely to make and, further, I never forgot the priest.

The dream I give is a fair sample of the type of analysis that took place and the kind of progress we were able to make. With regard to childhood situations I was able to loosen repressions a great deal without ever explicitly and directly speaking of sexual problems which would certainly have stopped the analysis, and it was interesting to find that even limited in this way her libido was loosened sufficiently to break through the heavy frost of repression as it did, though tentatively and timidly, when she made overtures to her husband.

The dream was this: " *She went into a church where she was sure the vicar was receiving birthday presents. She felt very peevish. She tried to put the cushions right in her pew and couldn't. She climbed over into another pew. A woman was nursing a baby. Then she saw a puddle on the floor and climbed back to her old pew at the back of the church but she found she was facing the audience for all that.*"

On the day of relating this dream she had arrived in a " bad " mood and on encouraging her to tell me to what she thought the " bad " feeling was due, she said she couldn't find any cause. True she had been annoyed the night before to find that her usual seat in the hotel lounge had been appropriated by a stranger who sat there quite unconcerned when she hovered round hoping he would take the hint and get out of it, and he didn't. The maid had been delayed in bringing her morning tea. More visitors, she had thought, and the residents who had been there longest, instead of being as they ought to be, thought of first, got neglected for the newcomers. It appeared too that her husband had had a visitor the night before and they talked together a great deal and had not seemed very anxious to hear what she had had to say.

She had been greatly astonished, she said, at what I had said the day before, that a child thinks anything about its " motions " at all. She didn't think a child would think about such dirty things. It was something that had to be done and she had assumed the child would be as glad to get it over and cleared away as the mother was. It was entirely a new idea to her and she felt rather disgusted when I had suggested the child might be interested. However she had recalled a time when she had been abroad staying with some new friends she had made. She had gone up to the child's nursery and the little girl was sitting on her pot, when her father, the professor, came in and, said the patient, " to my utter astonishment the professor bent down and kissed the child while sitting there and he said to her, ' Well, little one, and how are you getting on ? How much have you done ? ' The little girl was delighted and jumped up and said: ' Look, so much,' and the professor rejoined ' Good little girl.' " The patient said " I'd never seen or heard such a thing before. I didn't know how to take it, to be disgusted or what. But the child was pleased enough. My husband never behaved like that to any of our children, but there, I shouldn't have had him in the nursery to see things like that."

The patient then paused and said she couldn't think of more to say. I said: " Well, you told me a dream. Think of it, keep it in your mind, look at it as if you were looking at a picture and let it bring other pictures and thoughts if you can." Then she replied: " Those cushions and clambering about and sitting on the back pew, while I see myself doing that in the dream I am reminded of my own children. When there was one baby of course she sat opposite to me while I was wheeling the pram. Then we could see each other and talk. When the second baby came and he was taken out in the pram I put the first baby with its back to me and the new baby boy opposite to me, where the first baby used to be. I suppose from what has been talked about in the analysis on these matters I suppose that the first child doesn't like to be moved from its own seat, but I don't remember my own first child objecting any more than I remember myself objecting to my baby brother, but you have hinted that the child does object to being usurped."

To which I replied: "But you feel now just as you did then as a child." To which she said: "How is that possible ? I'm grown up, you are referring to babyhood."

I replied: "You resented the man who had taken your accustomed seat last night in the lounge." "Wasn't that natural ?" she replied. "Quite," I said, "as natural to think of a seat in an hotel as your own private property as it is for a first baby to think of its seat in a pram as its own and to resent the next baby taking it, and as natural to resent not being taken as much notice of when there is someone else who has to be entertained, as in the conversation last night, or again this morning when the new-comers were fed before you and you were kept waiting."

Two other interpretations I was able to give in light of other associations of this hour. One of these was a surmise that the dream held a repressed memory of urinating in her babyhood anger, and the second was a preliminary move on my part to connect with it the story of the little girl who pleased the professor by passing of motions as the child's first way of giving presents to her father. I drew an analogy between this and the phantasy of a little girl's wish to be able to do what the mother did, and I made a surmise that this dream concerned the time when her father was receiving the present of a baby from her mother. It was a " birthday " present. The transference situation was explained in this hour by the fact that the patient had been kept waiting five minutes the day before, and I could in this particular setting make use of the fact that the patient was lying as it were in the back seat, and so the phantasy of being kept waiting because of another child was the more complete.

This dream and the particulars of the type of case illustrates very well I think the problem of pace in an analysis, the necessity of following the pace set by the patient.

I shall finish this chapter by quoting a dream which gives a very clear picture of a child's problem in reality alongside the unconscious phantasy. This is the dream: " *I saw a genealogical table set out and it showed how characters in Jane Austen's novels were related to each other.*" The dreamer said in further elaboration " it was as if certain characters in one novel appeared again in another novel along with new ones, and this table showed how they were all related to each other." The " table," the patient said, was set out in the usual manner of genealogical tables showing different descendants with their marriages and children, so that it was possible to see all the different branches of the family and their progenitors.

Associations were first made to actual puzzling experiences. The dreamer as a little boy had this conundrum. X was his sister, Y was his sister and Z his brother. A was his brother and so was B, but the father of A and B was dead while the boy's own father was alive. Yet his mother was the mother of A and B. In the dream the relationships of all the characters was quite clear.

The dreamer chose an eminent woman novelist as a tribute to his own mother who created children who became distinguished in adult life.

Another puzzling situation was allied to this one presented by his brothers and sisters who had the same mother and different fathers. It was revealed by the fact that the genealogical table in the dream had in it some of the marks and signs that are familiar in a multiplication table. One then realized what a conundrum to a child the multiplication table can present. From this association to " multiplication " the patient turned his thoughts to procreation, and it became clear to me why some children have a difficulty in even comprehending that one and one make two. One and one may make half a dozen. In the instance I am giving you the problem was still more difficult. One and one had first made two. The father died and the mother survived. Then one and one had made four. When would the second father die ? And whom could his mother have then to make more children ? In the logic of this child's range of facts it was inevitable that the father must die after children had been created.

A further level of phantasy was revealed by the significance of the word " table." Why should it be a multiplication " table " ? The only meaning a " table " had to the little boy was a place for food. This in the child's own experience must always be a projection of the mother's body which is the first table from which is obtained the food supply. By this route of associations we reached

123

the first and simplest infantile phantasy that procreation is achieved by means of food.

Each patient has an individual psychology. The technique demanded of the analyst must be fashioned not only from the analyst's knowledge of the unconscious mind, but from his own ability to adapt himself to a specific individual. The problems of an individual are inseparable from special environmental factors and these are as important to know as any other if our technique is to be a subtler instrument than the yardstick which measures every type of cloth. Analytic technique is an applied art and as in all art its principles are conditioned by the limitations of its medium. The analyst's method of approach, tempo and interpretation must be in accordance with the specific personality of the patient. Oils and water colours, clay and stone, violin and piano, lyric and novel, could all portray one specific human emotion, but the technique of communication is very different. So in dealing with the emotions common to all mankind the perennial interest lies in their endless manifestations in individual settings. The nuances of technique, when the analyst is attuned to his material, will arise in response to the particular medium in which he works.

CHAPTER V

Analysis of a Single Dream

THIS chapter will be devoted to the consideration of all that was said by a patient during an hour in which a dream was related. I shall give a brief summary of the significant psychical events of the two analyses that followed this particular hour and the phase of analysis that developed from it, because only so can one gauge whether one's interpretations are helping to bring the repressed and suppressed emotional attitudes, phantasies or affective memories to conscious understanding.

The dream I have selected is not one that yielded up its significance as easily as did the example I gave of the woman who was in stress concerning micturition. Out of many possible interpretations I had to decide which I would select in order to focus attention upon them.

I am going to give one special aspect of this patient's problems very shortly in order to make the hour I speak of intelligible from the point of view of the stage the analysis had reached. In a case as complex as this one is I should confuse the issue by attempting to give you any account of it as a whole.

This is the phase at the moment of paramount importance. The patient's father died when he was three years of age. He was the youngest child. He has the dimmest of memories about his father, really only one of which he can fully say " I remember this." His father was much revered and beloved and the patient has only heard good and admirable things reported of him. So great had been the repression of unconscious problems associated with his father and his father's death that for nearly three years in analysis his references to his father were almost invariably to the fact that his father was dead. The emphasis has always been on " my father died," " is dead." It was a startling moment when one day he thought that his father had also lived, and still more startling when he thought that he must have heard his father speak. After that very slowly came the possibility of understanding the vicissitudes of the first three years of his life and the psychological changes that ensued on his father's death. Just as the psychical ties to his father have been bound by repression in the unconscious so the transference of those on to myself have remained unconscious. As his father has been " dead," so as far as the father transference has been concerned I have been " dead " too. He has no thoughts about me. He feels nothing about me. He cannot believe in the theory of transference. Only when he finishes at the end of a term, only when the week-ends come round, does he have a dim stirring of anxiety of some kind and only for the last month or so has he been able to entertain, even intellectually, the idea that this anxiety has anything to do with me or the analysis. He has persistently attributed it to some real cause he can always find to account for it.

I think the analysis might be compared to a long-drawn-out game of chess and that it will continue to be so until I cease to be the unconscious avenging father who is bent on cornering him, checkmating him, after which there is no alternative to death. The way out of this dilemma (for no one will surpass him in the technique of manœuvre since phantastically his life depends on it) is to bring slowly to light his unconscious wish of the first years to get rid of his father, for only this wish alive again in the transference will ever moderate his omnipotent belief that he killed his father in reality. It has to be tested again in the transference and against this all his ego-preservative instincts are enlisted. It is a bodily preservation for which he is phantastically struggling, not at the present even to save his penis; his penis and his body are one thing.

It is difficult in a most complicated set of interwoven problems to select one aspect of even one problem as a separate thing. Think of this problem of bodily preservation as it worked out in the patient's adult life. When the time came for him to practise at the bar he developed severe phobias. Put briefly this meant not that he dare not work successfully but that he must stop working in reality because he would be only too successful. His father's dying words, repeated to the little son, were: " Robert must take my place," and for Robert this meant that to grow up was also to die.

It also meant a re-enforcement of the unconscious phantasy of a devouring mother-imago whose love and care only ended in his father's death.

The task of analysis is to reduce the fear of the aggressive wishes experienced in his first three years. The terror of the aggressive wish and its phantastic consequences will be modified only by bringing this wish to consciousness, and only so will the libidinal wishes not continue to mean death. Moreover, since it is his body-ego that has to be preserved it will only be through or by phantasies of the body and the bodily functions that psychical development will be possible. I mean by this that the problems concern the body-ego. The psychical-ego can only be thin when its activities are engaged extensively to defend the body itself from phantastic extinction. Even his intellectual development is used at present mainly for defensive purposes. The acquirement of knowledge is driven by one main need. The problem of this patient is a bodily one and my task if I can accomplish it is to translate his long reasoned discourses into a bodily language. The problem concerning his actual body is that of repression of bodily feeling. He dreads " feeling." All his organized efforts have produced a marvellous control of muscle and movement, a control so established as to appear natural and inevitable, and his speech in the same way exhibits by its finish and diction the same discipline. The vital life is lost, the perfection is a dead perfection, even as his father's. One thing I never lose sight of in this analysis is, therefore, the chance of analysing abstractions into terms of bodily happenings. The second thing is that I do not concentrate on the major problem of his adult life, namely why cannot he work? when will he work? but on all those things that he can actually do, such as play tennis and golf, draw, paint and garden. For if his inhibitions and difficulties about these are resolved when the phantasies they reveal can be explored then they will lead on to an ability to work professionally. He calls these pursuits " only play." When they are really " only play " work will no longer be dangerous, for happy work is based on happy play.

On the day when the patient related to me the dream I have selected for this chapter I did not hear him coming upstairs. I never do. There is a carpet on the stairs, but that is not the reason. One patient comes up two stairs at a time and I hear just the extra thud; another hurries and I detect the hustle; another is sure to knock a suitcase or umbrella or fist on the banisters. One patient two out of three times blows his nose like a trumpet. One brings in hat, umbrella and suit-case. They have to be disposed of somewhere. One patient bangs them down on the first piece of furniture available. One carefully selects a place and puts his things down. One patient flings himself on the couch. One walks round to the farther side of the couch before lying down. One patient hesitates and looks round at the room before trusting himself on the couch at all. One lies still on the couch and then moves about when tired of one position. Another will roll about from the first moment and become comfortable and still as the hour proceeds.

But I never hear this patient on the stairs. He never brings his hat or coat or umbrella with him.

He never varies. He always gets on the couch one way. He always gives a conventional greeting with the same smile, a pleasant smile, not forced or manifestly covering hostile impulses. There is never anything as revealing as that would be. There is no sign of hurry, nothing haphazard, no clothes awry; no marks of a quick toilet; no hair out of place. The maid at home may have been late, his breakfast delayed, but these facts if I am lucky I may hear before the hour is over, and often I may hear them only the next day. He lies down and makes himself easy. He puts one hand over the other across his chest. He lies like that until the hour is over. Lately to my relief he has been able to scratch his nose or his ear when he has felt an irritation and a few weeks ago he even felt a sensation in the genitals. He talks the whole hour, clearly, fluently, in good diction, without hesitation and with many pauses. He speaks in a distinct and even voice for it expresses thinking and never feeling.

I have said I never hear him on the stairs, but for a few days prior to this hour just before he came into the room I had been aware of the smallest and discreetest of coughs. You will judge of the dearth of unconscious manifestations in bodily ways when I say my ear caught that tiny discreet cough with great joy. I made no reference to it hoping it might get louder. To draw this patient's attention to a manifestation of the unconscious is to stop it. His great aim is not to betray himself and to control anything that gives him away. Added to that is the fact that he becomes aware very quickly of any unconscious manifestation and so thwarts any spontaneity.

So on this day after the initial good-morning he lay down and said to my disappointment, in his customary even and deliberate voice: "I have been considering that little cough that I give just before I enter the room. The last few days I have coughed I have become aware of it, I don't know whether you have. To-day when the maid called me to come upstairs I made up my mind I would not cough. To my annoyance, however, I realized I had coughed just as I had finished. It is most annoying to do a thing like that, most annoying that something goes on in you or by you that you cannot control, or do not control. One would think some purpose is served by it, but what possible purpose can be served by a little cough of that description it is hard to think."

(*Analyst.*) What purpose could be served?

(*Patient.*) Well, it is the kind of thing that one would do if one were going into a room where two lovers were together. If one were approaching such a place one might cough a little discreetly and so let them know they were going to be disturbed. I have done that myself when, for example, I was a lad of fifteen and my brother was with his girl in the drawing-room I would cough before I went in so that if they were embracing they could stop before I got in. They would not then feel as embarrassed as if I had caught them doing it.

(*Analyst.*) And why cough before coming in here?

(*Patient.*) That is absurd, because naturally I should not be asked to come up if someone were here, and I do not think of you in that way at all. There is no need for a cough at all that I can see.

It has, however, reminded me of a phantasy I had of being in a room where I ought not to be, and thinking someone might think I was there, and then I thought to prevent anyone from coming in and finding me there I would bark like a dog. That would disguise my presence. The " someone " would then say, " Oh, it's only a dog in there."

(*Analyst.*) A dog ?

(*Patient.*) That reminds me of a dog rubbing himself against my leg, really masturbating himself. I'm ashamed to tell you because I did not stop him. I let him go on and someone might have come in. (The patient then coughed.)

I do not know why I should now think of my dream last night. It was a tremendous dream. It went on for ages and ages. It would take me the rest of the hour to relate it all. But don't worry; I shall not bore you with it all for the simple reason that I cannot recall it. But it was an exciting dream, full of incident, full of interest. I woke hot and perspiring. It must have been the longest dream I ever had. I dreamt *I was taking a journey with my wife around the world, and we arrived in Czechoslovakia where all kinds of things were happening. I met a woman on a road, a road that now reminds me of the road I described to you in the two other dreams lately in which I was having sexual play with a woman in front of another woman.* So it happened in this dream. *This time my wife was there while the sexual event occurred. The woman I met was very passionate looking* and I am reminded of a woman I saw in a restaurant yesterday. She was dark and had very full lips, very red and passionate looking, and it was obvious that had I given her any encouragement she would have

132

responded. She must have stimulated the dream, I expect. In the dream the *woman wanted intercourse with me and she took the initiative which as you know is a course which helps me a great deal.* If the woman will do this I am greatly helped. In the dream *the woman actually lay on top of me; that has only just come to my mind. She was evidently intending to put my penis in her body. I could tell that by the manœuvres she was making. I disagreed with this, but she was so disappointed I thought that I would masturbate her.* It sounds quite wrong to use that verb transitively. One can say " I masturbated " and that is correct, but it is all wrong to use the word transitively.

(*Analyst.*) To use the *verb* transitively is " all wrong ? "

(*Patient.*) I see what you mean. It is true I have only masturbated myself.

(*Analyst.*) Only ?

(*Patient.*) I only remember masturbating another boy once and I forget all the details and I feel shy about mentioning it. That is the only time I can remember. The dream is in my mind vividly. There was no orgasm. I remember her vagina gripped my finger. I see the front of her genitals, the end of the vulva. Something large and projecting hung downwards like a fold on a hood. Hoodlike it was, and it was this that the woman made use of in manœuvring to get my penis. The vagina seemed to close round my finger. The hood seemed strange.

(*Analyst.*) What else do you think of—let the look of it be in your mind.

(*Patient.*) I think of a cave. There is a cave on the hillside where I lived as a child. I often went there with my mother. It is visible from the road along which one walks. Its most remarkable feature is that it has an overhanging top to it which looks very much like a huge lip. I used to think it was like a monster lip when I was a child. I suddenly think labia means lips. There is some joke about the labia running crosswise and not longitudinally, but I don't remember how the joke was arranged, some comparison between Chinese writing and our own, starting from different sides, or from bottom to top. Of course the labia are side by side, and the vagina walls are back and front, that is, one longitudinal and the other crosswise. I'm still thinking of the hood.

(*Analyst.*) Yes, how now ?

(*Patient.*) A funny man at one of the earliest golf courses I remember. He said he could get me a golf bag cheaply and the material would be " motor hood cloth." It was the accent I remember. I shall never forget it. (Imitates it.) Imitating him like that reminds me of a friend who broadcasts impersonations which are very clever, but it sounds " swank " to tell you, as swanky as telling you what a marvellous wireless set I have. It picks up all stations with no difficulty.

My friend has a splendid memory. She remembers her childhood too, but mine is so bad below eleven years. I do remember, however, one of the earliest songs we heard at the theatre and she imitated the man afterwards. It was " Where did you get that hat, where did you get that tile ? " My mind has gone to the hood again and I am remembering the first car I was ever in, but of course they were called motors then when they were new. I remember the hood of it, that's " motor hood " again you see. Well! the hood of this motor was one of its most obvious features. It was strapped back when not in use. The inside of it was lined with scarlet. The peak of speed for that car was about sixty, as much as is good for the life of a car. Strange how one speaks of the life of a car as if it were human. I remember I was sick in that car, and that reminds me of the time I had to urinate into a paper bag when I was in a railway train as a child. Still I think of the hood.

(*Analyst.*) You said straps held it back?

(*Patient.*) Yes, of course, that makes me think of how I used to collect leather straps, of how I used to cut up leather straps. I thought I wanted the strips to make something useful but I expect something quite unnecessary. I dislike thinking it was a compulsion; that's why the cough annoys me. I suppose I cut up my sister's sandals in the same way. I have only the dimmest memory of doing it. I don't know why nor what I wanted the leather for when I had done it.

But I suddenly thought of straps that one sees a child fastened by in a " pram " and immediately I wanted to say there was no " pram " in our family, and I then thought how silly you are, you must have had a " pram." I can't recall it any more than I can remember seeing my father in his invalid chair being wheeled about, though I have a vague memory of seeing the chair.

I've suddenly remembered I meant to send off letters admitting two members to the Club. I boasted of being a better secretary than the last and yet here I am forgetting to give people permission to enter the Club. " Ah well, we have undone those things we ought to have done and there is no good thing in us."

(*Analyst.*) Undone ?

(*Patient.*) Well, I was going to say that that phrase made me think of " fly buttons," which I never leave undone, never forget, but to my astonishment last week my wife noticed I had. It was at dinner and I surreptitiously did them up under the table. And I recall now a dream in which you remember a man was telling me to fasten up my coat buttons. This reminds me of straps again and of how as a child I had to be pinned in bed at night lest I should fall out. I expect I was strapped in the pram too.

I will now review the recurring themes of the latent thoughts in the order as they appeared.

1. The cough.
2. Ideas concerning the purpose of a cough.

   (a) Brings thoughts of lovers being together.
   (b) Rejection of sexual phantasy concerning analyst.
   (c) Phantasy of being where he ought not to be, and barking like a dog to put people off the scent.
   (d) Dog again brought memory of masturbating a dog.

At this juncture he coughed (compare with bark) and suddenly he remembered the dream.

3. The next theme was the dream. In the recital of this was the vivid picture of the actual woman he saw with (*a*) full lips, (*b*) The dream woman's

vulva with a projection like a hood which she was using in some manœuvre to get his penis. This occurred on a road associated in his mind with two dreams in which he was having sexual play with a woman in the presence of another.

During the recital while telling about the sexual play in the dream he objected to using the verb " masturbate " transitively; " it seemed all wrong."

4. The next theme was that of the hood; leading him to remember the cave and the overhanging top of the cave which was like a lip.

5. Then he passed from labia and lips to ideas of things running cross-wise and longitudinal and a joke he could not remember. He thought again of " hood."

6. The next theme came via hood to motor-hood cloth remembered because of a man's accent. He imitated this accent himself.

7. This brought him to his friend's clever impersonations and a particular one of impersonating a man. He deprecated his " swank " about his friend as he did about his marvellous wireless set. Her memory and his *bad one* (now remembers).

8. He went back to " hood " again and remembered the first car he was ever in. It had a hood lined with scarlet which was strapped up. He was sick in the car and then he remembered urinating as a child in the train.

9. The " hood " with straps recalled a period in his childhood when he compulsively cut up leather straps and on one occasion his sister's sandals.

10. Straps made him think of children strapped

in prams. He inferred he must have had a pram. There had been two children older than himself.

11. He remembered he had not sent tickets admitting new members to the Club. He had left undone those things he should have done.

12. Leaving fly buttons undone.

13. The dream in which he was told " to button up."

14. He returned then to straps and remembered being told that he used to be pinned in bed lest he fell out, and supposes he was strapped in the pram too.

The first thing of importance is to find the cardinal clue to the significance of the dream. We can do that by noting just the moment when it came to the patient's mind. He had been speaking of the incident of a dog masturbating on his leg. The moment before he had been speaking of imitating a dog himself, that is, he identified himself with dog. Then he gave a cough. Then he remembered the dream, a long and exciting dream from which he awoke hot and perspiring. The deduction concerning the significance of the whole dream is that it is a masturbation phantasy. That is of first importance. The next thing to notice in connection with this masturbation phantasy is the theme of potency. He is travelling round the world. It is the longest dream he has ever had. It would take a whole hour to relate. Correlate with that his deprecation of " swank " regarding his friend's impersonations which are broadcast to the world, and his own wireless set which picks up every station. Note his own imitation of the man whose accent attracted him, a strong colloquial accent, and incidentally he said with regard to this man " he had once been a butcher."

Impersonation here, whether via friend or himself, has the significance of imitating a stronger or better-known person. This is again a further clue to the meaning of the masturbation phantasy, that is, a phantasy in which he is impersonating another person, one of immense power and potency.

The next question that arises from that is why this phantasy of extreme power ? The answer is given in the dream. He is going round the world. I would put as commensurate with this idea the actual memory that came to him when he was describing the hood in the dream which was so strange, for it brought out not only the fact that he was describing a projection, a fold of a hood, but that the hood was also overhanging like a lip of a cave. So that we get directly the hood and lips of the vulva compared with the great cave on the hillside to which he went with his mother. Hence the masturbation phantasy is one associated with immense potency because he is dreaming of compassing mother earth, of being adequate to the huge cave beneath the protruding lips. That is the second thing of importance.

Next I would draw your attention to the associations concerning lips and labia. The woman who was a stimulus for the dream had full red passionate lips. In the dream he had a vivid picture of the labia and the hood. The cave had an overhanging lip. He thinks of things longitudinal like labia and then of cross-wise things—where I would now suggest the mouth as compared with the vulva.

He thinks, moreover, of the first motor he was in and of its hood and of the scarlet lining in that motor. He then thinks immediately of the speed of the car, and says " the peak of its speed " was so many miles an hour, and then speaks of " the life of the car " and notices that he talks of a car as if it were human.

From the fact of the dream picture of the vulva and the hood, with the wealth of other associations that give the picture of " red inside " and projecting lips and hood I should deduce that the memory of the actual cave which he visited with his mother also acts as a cover memory. I would deduce that there is projected on to the motor with its scarlet lined hood this same forgotten memory and that the peak of speed has the same significance as the projection in the genitals in the dream—it is the peak of the hood. I infer there is an actual repressed memory of seeing the genitals of someone much older than himself; of seeing them when he was very tiny and I infer this from both the car and the cave and going round the world in conjunction with the immense potency required. The peak, the hood, I interpret as the clitoris. The patient's sister is eight years older than himself. Considering the references made to his woman friend's voice, that is to sound, accent, sound of a man's voice, and considering that the reference to her is in connection with male impersonation, I deduce that at least when very tiny he saw her genitals, noticed the clitoris, and heard her urinate. But considering all the work in analysis we have done so far I believe in addition there was some babyhood situation in which he had a quite definite opportunity of seeing his mother's genitals. I mean by this, some situation such as might occur by a child being laid on the floor on a blanket. It is the only explanation I have up to the present of understanding the special importance of certain lightings that this patient favours in making pictures, namely lighted from below. One more clue I have to the woman in the dream is that she is dark. His actual selection among women has been the blonde and golden-hair type. He has on previous occasions told me that his mother was dark-haired and that he has always correlated passion in woman with dark hair.

The next thing of importance is the evidence afforded of childhood masturbation. We have the recall of the dream in which he is told to button up and the fact that this dream is remembered in conjunction with the memory of being pinned in bed. This he says was to prevent his falling out of bed. In connection with this I correlate material from other analyses in which he has told me that he was pinned in bed because he was " so restless " and also that on occasions he has remarked that he can think of nothing so infuriating to a child as to be hampered in movement, restricted in any way, but he did not know why he felt so sure about this as he never remembered any time when he was not allowed freedom. From these references to " straps " and " being pinned in bed," one is justified in deducing some restriction of his movements in early childhood connected with masturbation, and that this early masturbation was in its phantasy content of the same nature as the present-day dream.

We can now proceed with further details. We

have two references to compulsion. The first is in connection with the "little" cough which in spite of effort he does involuntarily—a fact which is extremely distasteful to him. The other is the reference to the early boyhood compulsion of cutting straps, the cutting up of his sister's sandals. Very reluctantly he has admitted that this cutting was compulsively done. The point to notice in the reference to this compulsive aggressiveness is the sequence in which it occurs, namely straps, straps of a pram, refusal to think there was a pram, then the thought that there must have been a pram, then that there had been other children before him, and finally at that point he remembered that he had forgotten to send tickets to two new members of the Club. This sequence gives us the right to interpret that his difficulty in remembering that there was a pram which he must have had and as he says "there were other children" was due to his not wanting his mother to have other children after himself, and further that his early aggression exhibited in "cutting" was definitely aggression towards the possible and hated rivals. The present-day manifestation of this is to neglect to send tickets to admit new members. The childhood phantasy was to cut them up or cut them out.

We can make still further inferences. Immediately he mentioned the fact that he had forgotten to send these tickets of admission he said: "We have left undone those things we ought to have done" and he was reminded of the fact that quite recently a most unusual thing happened: he found his fly buttons were unfastened. The unconscious wish to exhibit his penis is implicit in this "forgetting,"

142

but taken in its setting in the sequence of references first to aggressiveness by the cutting, then to not sending tickets, the penis is unconsciously associated with phantasies of aggression. I am justified here by virtue of past analyses in linking up aggressive phantasies connected with the penis, not only with masturbation, but with bed-wetting, since the restlessness referred to which caused his being pinned in bed has also been spoken of in connection with bed-wetting on previous occasions. You will notice that by this reference to leaving his fly buttons undone he recalled a dream where a father-figure exhorted him to fasten up his buttons.

This leads me to a further inference. In speaking of the cough his first thought was of warning two lovers of his approach. He remembered warning in this way his brother and a girl friend when they were together. One knows what this warning will bring about before the younger brother gets into the room. The lovers will have put some distance between themselves. He will by his cough have separated them. To use his words: "Then they will not be embarrassed by my intrusion." Now again I am justified in my surmise concerning this extreme solicitude not to be embarrassing. Some time ago he attended a function at which the King and Queen were to be present. He came up to town in his car. He developed anxiety about this and for some time it was not clear what specific phantasy was the reason of it. It turned out to be this: "Suppose, not knowing exactly where he would park the car, suppose just at the moment the King and Queen were arriving he blocked the way with his car and could not get it to move, and

143

so hindered the progress of the royal pair—a most embarrassing situation."

So that in the discreet cough before he enters the room we have the pale attenuated representation of an infantile situation in which he hindered the progress of the royal pair, not by discretion, not by immobility, but by sudden movement of his bowels, or by crying, which one infers was effectual in its purpose.

With regard to one specific detail in the dream, namely the projection which he thinks the woman is manœuvring to get hold of his penis, one is justified in going as far in interpretation as this: namely that in light of the aggressive phantasies that have been evinced the woman's genitals will be aggressive towards him. Note the actual danger places: (1) the projection which is equivalent to a penis, (2) the vagina. He will not trust his penis in the vagina, he will put in a finger. Moreover, the mouth and vagina have been equated through the association of "over-hanging lips" and in the reference to the longitudinal and cross-wise openings; hence we have here the phantasy of the vagina being like the mouth with teeth.

To interpret more than this would be to guess. The actual interpretations I have given arise directly out of the material of the hour either by direct association, or by noticing the setting of the thoughts in sequences, or by connection of the associations in this hour with those given in another.

This is the attempt to get the full significance of everything said.

I did not interpret to the patient as I have done here. I had to select from the whole what was the most important thing to help towards bringing the repressed material into consciousness. I was guided in selection by the patient's need, namely his fear of aggressive bodily movements. The thing I selected first was the cough. I selected it because it was the one direct transference manifestation of a compulsive nature made during the hour which could in any way make a link with the repressed compulsive aggressive acts of childhood.

I referred to the fact that he had twice used the word " little " in describing his cough and said that by using this word he was under-estimating a phantasy connected with the cough. I referred then specifically to the dream and pointed out how the dream as a whole indicated immense power, great potency.

Then I directed his attention to the purpose of the cough in the direct reference to separating lovers and said some phantasy of that kind must now be unconsciously associated with myself. He had said that he would not bore me by a long recital. I then referred to the " King and Queen " incident and surmised that the omnipotent phantasy was rooted in early infancy where he had been able to stop or interrupt his parents.

After this I correlated the associations made to aggression and deduced that he had wished to prevent any more children being born; because there had been no more children born after him his aggressive phantasy of omnipotence had been reinforced by this fact, and thus further enhanced his dread of his mother, as a revenging person. I then affirmed my conviction of his actual sight of his mother's genitals and the projection on to them

145

of revenge phantasies which were to be correlated with the phantasies of aggression associated with his own penis as a biting and boring thing, and with the power of his water. All this I said was the significance of the masturbation which the dream represented.

Now I will indicate very briefly what were the outstanding features of the two following hours of analysis.

The next day the patient said that he had not coughed coming up the stairs, but that he had had a slight colicky pain. This led him to think of his attacks of diarrhœa in childhood and that with colic there is very often explosive flatus. " I wonder," he said, " if the cough really meant wind and diarrhœa ?" I replied, " Now you have found its meaning for yourself." During this hour he was occupied by the problem of his difficulty in tennis in putting a shot just so that it should corner his opponent.

The following day he informed me that he had had a colicky pain on leaving the house the day before. Then he proceeded to tell me that he had been unable to use his car because certain repairs had not been finished. The garage man was so very good, so very kind; it was impossible to be angry with him. Still he would like to have his car. Not that the car was imperative for him at the moment; it was not a necessity, but he wanted it, he liked it.

At this juncture I drew a comparison between the kind and good garage man with whom he could not get angry and his father. This the patient said exactly expressed his feelings about his father in

146

memory. Then for once I was able to deal with the libidinal wishes, " not that the car was a necessity, but he wanted it." I have had to wait a long time for the chance to make this interpretation. Here at last libidinal desire was expressed. On the following day the patient had a confession to make. For the first time since he was a tiny boy he had wet the bed during sleep.

Thus in these three analytic hours the bodily manifestations in order were the cough, colic pains, and actual bed-wetting. With this last we had made the first real contact with the rivalry situation with his father in infancy.

In this hour I was able to speak convincingly of the father transference as evinced in the analysis, and the aggressive rival phantasies towards him that in infancy were expressed in bodily ways.

I missed a chance at one spot of asking for more information, an obvious omission, although with this patient I do not interrupt more than is necessary for progress. I refer to the element in the dream of " Czechoslovakia."

Finally you will understand why I said so little, why I interpolated few questions and those couched in almost monosyllables. The reason is given in his dream and his remark " The woman took the initiative. If the woman will only take the initiative then I am greatly helped," which means that his problem of infantile aggression is shelved again. To help this patient I must on occasions of this kind let him take the initiative as far as I can make it possible.

Two dreams in which definite father-figures appeared followed the one I have given. On the tennis court one day in the week that followed this analytic hour an opponent who beat him began to tease him about his poor play. My patient got hold of his tormentor round his neck and held him playfully in a strangle grip and warned him never to tease him again. This is the first time since he was an adolescent that he has been able to touch a man in any kind of playful way at all—still less to make a demonstration of his physical strength.

CHAPTER VI

Problems in Dream Analysis

1. Characteristic affect preceding a dream that brought to consciousness a repressed memory.
2. Dreams embodying (a) repressed memories; (b) phantasies.
3. The value of knowing the stimulus to a dream: (a) external to analysis; (b) within the analysis.

I PROPOSE to devote this chapter to a variety of problems connected with analysis of dreams.

Repressed unconscious conflicts may be thought of as: (1) conflicts concerning things we should like to have done prompted by our infantile love impulses, by our hate impulses, but could not and did not perform; (2) conflicts concerning the disasters that occurred in childhood which because of hate impulses we have unconsciously attributed to our infantile omnipotence as, for example, the death of parents, brothers and sisters, or their illnesses and misfortunes; (3) conflicts concerning things which to us in our lack of knowledge were disasters but which were not so actually, such as, for example, the female genitals and menstruation. These natural phenomena can be thought of as disasters because of guilt concerning infantile agression; (4) conflicts concerning things we have actually done in our past. These are interwoven with the loves and hates of infancy so that all the different types of disaster I have mentioned, phantastic and real, become associated with childhood activities innocuous as most of these really are. I find myself inclined to put the emphasis on the *positive* experiences of the patient, as, for example, bodily sensation of any kind painful and pleasant and actual happenings in response to inner and outer stimuli. We may sometimes have to approach the repressed actual experience via phantasy first; sometimes it is so, sometimes it is not. We must take the material as it comes, but even the infantile omnipotent phantasy that inhibits an adult patient from working in reality has its setting in an infantile practical situation about which a phantasy is rooted that has never been subjected to adult reality. I mean, for example, on occasions an infant is able actually to separate his parents and control them to his own immediate ends.

An omnipotent phantasy in the unconscious mind can supply the driving power necessary for accomplishing good work in real life but I am concerned here with the terror of omnipotence that thwarts and spoils life energies. In the case I mentioned I should myself ultimately hope to find not only the phantasy of separating the parents but some practical basis for it, such as a bed-wetting or a screaming which accomplished an actual separation. The behaviour of the parents due to their own psychological reactions on such occasions will constitute an environmental factor that will increase or mitigate the child's fear of its omnipotent phantasy life. My own search always seems to be for the exercise of the child's senses themselves, the child's sense experiences, the child's activities and the correlation of these with the phantasies constructed in that dim reality period.

Phantasy and reality, if we can find the psychological moment, are two facets of a total experience and we can neglect neither if we are to know the whole truth.

Now in the analysis of a dream it may be that the principal gain in one hour is a childhood phantasy, but even then I should consider this only of partial value. In the actual associations we shall have references to real situations. The stimulus to a dream, it is worth noting is a real stimulus of the present day, which is consonant with the earliest infantile situation where life begins with an external as well as an internal stimulus. If an hour is mainly occupied by recovery of phantasy or elucidation of phantasy through a dream I should reserve in my mind the unsolved problem of where and how this phantasy is linked with actual repressed situations and how this is being re-staged in the transference setting.

I shall now give a practical illustration of a repressed affective memory returning to consciousness.

A patient related this dream. *She saw a huge ocean liner in dock and by the side of it was a huge airship.* She said she saw the rug on my hearth as a huge thing when she lay on the couch but when she stood up and looked down on it then it was smaller. She remembered during this hour's analysis a trade symbol of a ship which had underneath it a triangle the point of which was upwards and touching the ship. She said: " I see no point of connection between the triangle and the ship." I pointed out that her dream made ship and airship lie side by side so that there was no connection between them but that in the real trade symbol there was one. Possible also was the interpretation of wish-fulfilment, since in her dream she had made two " symbols " lie side by side while in reality there had been a connection between them. She said, " Yes, I see," quite cheerfully. She approved. " Very ingenious of my mind to put it like that."

This kind of hour is a preliminary one. I keep in mind the fact that she has actually seen a trade symbol of a ship and point of triangle in connection. No one but a wild analyst would say to the patient that because she saw that trade symbol she once saw her parents in intercourse. Nevertheless her dream denies what the actual trade symbol affirms. My deduction is that just because she is intensely occupied with reality I must be aware of her denial of reality.

A week later the analytic situation presented a great contrast. The patient lay on the couch in an exhausted condition. She complained of great fatigue. She had felt fatigued for days and could not think of a reason. As a matter of fact she had been to bed earlier than usual. She was menstruating but menstruation " never used to cause all this trouble. It was always a nuisance but I never felt it knock me out as it has done the last two months. It is now always regular whereas once it was always late, but with this greater regularity I'm feeling it much more, and I'm good for nothing." She lay unusually inert. She idly thought of going out for dinner the next night. She played with a button and then remembered a button was off the coat she was going to wear the following evening. X wouldn't approve if she wore a coat with a button off. He was immaculate himself. Her voice got slower and slower; she yawned, stretched, sighed and finally lay still, a picture of fatigue. For a time I said nothing. She gave a dry little cough that I know very well, a cough that has nothing to do with cold, catarrh, or huskiness. Time and again she coughed. I said, so that the pause should not be discouraging, " You are finding it difficult to-day." She replied, " I can't think of anything to talk about, only how weary I feel." " Sometimes," I said, " when it is like this a dream may have been forgotten." This remark was followed by an out-burst of coughing. Finally she exclaimed, " Why, yes, I did dream, if only I can remember it. It was very short. *I seemed to be in the country. There was grass and a whitewashed building. It was very lofty and I was in it, upstairs I think, a funny place and as if there might be a hole in the middle of the floor.*"

We now had twenty minutes of the hour left. The patient in that twenty minutes coughed practically before every sentence she uttered. The gist of that twenty minutes' work was this: The lofty building turned out to be an actual loft she remembered in the country place where she spent her holidays as a little girl. Then she recalled picking apples in an orchard with one of the boys living at the place. There had been a scrimmage and a chase by another boy. Then the guilty pair sought refuge in the loft and stayed there a long time. The patient coughed vigorously. Then she said: " I remember he put my hand through his trousers but I don't remember feeling his penis.

153

Then he put his hand under my clothes and he felt my stays, you know the kind of stays a little girl wears. He said: ' How many buttons you have on them, what are they for ? ' and I felt so ashamed."

Now I helped her. I did not want to risk her telling me a lie. I did not want her to forgo the triumph of finally overcoming her resistances. I remembered the " whitewash " on the lofty building. I remembered the denial of the week before in the dream of airship and ship and the trade symbol " I see no connection between them." I remembered that she will not believe there was any " connection " between her parents so long as she blots out real situations of her own life. So I said: " You have been tired these last days because there has been a struggle concerning this memory. It has been striving for recognition but the condemning part of your mind has been trying to keep it back. The energy has all been taken up in this fight." I pointed out her references to buttons in the analysis and that X would disapprove if she had one missing. He was so perfect, so immaculate. I said, without surmise (a surmise I do not hesitate to express when I am not sure of a thing), " One day I am sure you will be able to fill in that memory more definitely. The evidence is that you felt his penis and he felt your vulva." She said cautiously, and " Do you get it from the dream ? " I said, " Well, you said there was a hole in the middle of the loft floor, didn't you ? " She replied, " There always is in a loft," and I said: " Always too in a little girl, only for some reason you only think of buttons." I made at the end of the hour a reference to her menstrual period, saying that I thought phantastic reasons for bleeding were linked both with this incident as well as with others not yet known.

This hour's analysis exhibited many of the signs of an authentic memory struggling to consciousness. There were two or three days of analysis in which nothing of importance emerged at all, following on the " ship and aeroplane " dream, an obviously increasing resistance during which I had to bide my time. Then came physical fatigue, the cough, and in addition a thing I have omitted from my account, a sudden soreness and smarting of the eyes as the patient related the dream.

The next day the patient was as lively as ever. The physical effects had disappeared, so had the depression she had been feeling. This experience is typical with this patient. I know when a repressed memory is coming to consciousness but I do not think it is typical of her alone. Over and over again when phases of fatigue, listlessness, inability to remember ordinary things, inability to find things to say, appear during analysis I find them a prelude to the struggling into dreams and consciousness of affective memories. It is a very useful thing to remember when phases of resistance like these occur that this intra-psychical struggle absorbs energy and that the time factor must be taken into account and that this time factor differs with different patients.

I have been asked how one can differentiate between a phantasy coming to consciousness and an actual memory. Is there any need to trouble about the differentiation ? If one gets the phantasy, that is, the unconscious wish, has one not then got the dynamics of the situation ? There are certainly dynamic phantasies which could never be realities, but I still think the most phantastic if they *are* dynamic will be connected with some type of sense experience. I always endeavour as analysis proceeds to find the real basis of the phantasy, the transference providing the link between the present day and the bygone infantile situation. The effective emotional discharge is made possible in this way. I will illustrate my way of judging whether I am listening to phantasy or to the prelude of a memory.

A patient had a dream of " *a door in a garden wall.*" She thought of an actual door in a remembered garden. From that memory the patient proceeded to construct a phantasy of a gardener exposing himself. Now this might have been phantasy only and if phantasy then it would be the staging of a wish. It might have been actual memory but the patient herself could not remember such a scene. Now if a repressed memory were slowly coming to consciousness one would be certain that over a period of time this garden and door would appear over and over again in dreams or associations. The intervals between such references might be considerable but they would inevitably recur if there were a repressed real incident connected with this place.

If there is no recurrence of the theme " door in a garden wall " then I should conclude that " the gardener exposing himself" is a phantasy, but I should also expect to find some real basis for the phantasy. Compare this with the criteria in the following examples: Two patients over a period of twelve months dreamt of " sand " several times.

156

These dreams in every case led to thoughts of seeing a man's penis and of incontinence of urine, but there was no emergence of any actual memory. Still the very recurrence of these dreams, always with one psychological content, led me to conclude that memories of actual incidents were repressed. A dream will state and restate the same theme until the solution is reached.

Take another evidence of repressed memory material. *A patient dreamt of finding a round object under a pillow.* Associations led the patient to say that it was " red inside and white outside." The patient was in an anxious state. She described her feelings as " bloody." Finally in view of the hour's work I said I believed she once touched a rolled-up sanitary towel and that she was frightened at what she found. This patient was not satisfied. " Why do you say that is a memory, and yet we thought such and such might be a memory and might not ? Why do you say this is one ? "

My reason for being definite in this instance was not because this dream had occurred many times. It was because in the past she had refused to secure her sanitary towels and hated to tie tape round herself. The consequence was that there was a risk of the towel falling off and this risk led in reality to its once being dropped. She let fall something to frighten others as she was once frightened herself.

I have often had the experience of a patient starting an hour with a great outburst of anxiety, explosive anger, recrimination, criticism and self-criticism in connection with which one has only been able to elucidate the problem by a dream

157

given later in the hour. I am not thinking now of anxieties which one can predicate will occur through one's knowledge of the problems that are being brought to light. What I refer to is the reaching of a whole repressed affective incident or situation which because of the analytic work done in connection with resistances has nearly reached consciousness as far as memory is concerned, but the affect comes first. When the dream is told, and the memory recalled of some event that provoked great anger and grief, then one finds that the explosive anxiety and anger discharged in relation to the analyst is the affect of the actual incident brought up to date in the analysis. With patients of marked spontaneity, who feel first and then later think and recollect, one finds in the process of recovering actual early affective incidents that for a space of time the patient finds it quite impossible to think of the analyst as other than the real person in childhood with whom the affective incident occurred. It is the dream to which I am drawing your attention here. A great burst of anxiety that occurs at the beginning of a session which does not naturally follow from the analytic work of the previous day means: (1) some present-day stimulus exacerbating anxiety has yet to be related to the analyst, or (2) some past emotional event has become accessible and is inherent in a dream yet to be told.

I am not referring here to a prolonged anxiety state where early levels of phantasy and reality experiences are being worked through, but with spasmodic and recurrent anxiety outbursts.

Actual primal scenes and events of the earliest

infancy are matters of reconstruction, valid when dreams, associations, transference, affects and behaviour in the external world pile up evidence that admits of definite interpretation. There will generally be no actual memory. But I find also that affective memories up to the fourth and fifth year must often be reconstructed from dream material and phantasies and transference affects. Later than this age memories are of course repressed, but when released are more likely to come back as a whole incident. The kind of reconstruction I am here thinking of is of the following type. The " sand " appeared and reappeared in one patient's dreams. Then for a time I noted that her dreams introduced " steps." Then followed " wheels." Now all these elements had their own validity symbolically or in a real setting in the hour's analysis in which they occurred. But there came a day when these elements of sand, steps, wheels, fused into one thing, namely a bathing-van, and then I was able to predicate an actual repressed incident associated with the bathing-van.

I will give one or two dreams that are typical of phantasy. A patient reported that in a *dream she was crossing a paved courtyard with her head bowed and her arms crossed over her breast. She was filled with a spirit of quiet exaltation and said softly to herself: " I will graciously deign to be the mother of us all."* This was a Madonna phantasy. The dreamer will " graciously deign " provided she is the mother of God, not Joseph's wife.

Here is another dream. *The patient dreamt she was a child walking slowly along a corridor in a great mansion.*

She had heard a great hero had returned from the wars. He was in her bed in one of the rooms. She slightly lifted up the latch of the door and peeped into the room, a palatial room in which the bed was at the far end. She could see the hero sitting up in bed looking very fine and noble. She must get nearer, and slowly and quietly she tiptoed across the room until she stood at the end of the bed and gazed through the bars at him with adoration.

One was able to find the actual setting of this phantasy. The figure of the hero, the palatial rooms, the theme of the housing of a noble stranger were traceable to pictures and stories known in childhood. The dream child gives a perfect picture of the normal Œdipus situation.

Here is another. *The patient in the dream was standing in a room face to face with a wizard.* The wizard was traceable to a fairy-tale book of childhood. In the analysis I had a full description of the wizard, and how detail by detail the dream wizard was the book wizard come to life. He had a threatening attitude, and, said my patient, " the wizard was always the enemy of the prince, who finally killed him."

The meaning of the phantasy was clear enough in terms of symbolism but it was not until the patient gave me an actual occurrence of the day before, that I could make an interpretation that carried any weight. The stimulus of the dream was the meaning of the dream. The patient had been helping his wife into bed. Her night-dress got pulled up. He was straightening it for her, and on a sudden impulse he lifted it up and bending down over her he said playfully, " Hello, bogy."

He remembered this only at the end of the hour and then when I repeated the word "bogy" in a voice of inquiry he said, "Well, I never thought any more about it, but of course a bogy is a spirit, a ghost. I think of my father now. I expect that is the dream of the wizard in the room."

This leads me to another point in dream analysis that is worth considering, namely the present-day stimulus of the dream. I question very much whether the stimulus can be thought of as indifferent. It may be a trifle in reality, something to which we pay no conscious attention but a stimulus is such because of its psychical significance. Countless times the stimulus of a dream will not come to light, but when it does, I find it of great help in elucidating the dream. Think of this last example I have given and the life and cogency in the interpretation after he told me of that sudden impulse to say " Hello, bogy."

So again in an example like the following it is the stimulus of the dream that makes the sudden liveliness in the analytic work. The patient *dreamt she was at the Zoo, and " there was something about a meal*." She proceeded naturally enough to remember childhood visits to the Zoo, and of seeing the animals being fed. Sometimes she was not allowed to see the animals fed, and there were many things mother would not allow her to see and to do. The patient spent a long time enumerating all the " not alloweds " of her forbidding mother in childhood and then finished by suddenly saying " and elephants ? Did we see elephants, ride on elephants ? " There was a pause, and then she said,

161

" Last night I had such fun swishing a hose-pipe round, doing what I liked with it, making the water go where I wanted and finally trying to drink from it."

There in the stimulus is the meaning of the dream, alive and real, and the forbidding mother has given place to a picture of a lively and rebellious child, to say nothing of the phantasies this play of the previous night dramatized.

The stimuli of present-day life and dreams may be compared with stimuli of the past and early reactions to the external world. Take as a typical example the patient who started the hour by saying she was cross and then went on to a list of grievances about not getting her seat in the lounge and her breakfast tea at the right time. We do not have to search for this type of stimulus to dreams. They are soon revealed because the provocation proceeds from another person. But I believe many a baffling dream, many an obscure analytical hour, becomes clear once we have found a stimulus in connection with a present-day event where the patient either consciously or unconsciously has been himself the cause of provocation, or wished to be so. The present-day stimulus, action, or wish is suppressed because the repressed wish, actions, feelings are not yet realized and acknowledged.

I have been dealing here exclusively with stimuli received outside the analysis because it is in the external world that the patient is living as a psychical whole, acting and reacting as an individual entity. It is for this reason that external stimuli are important. By finding external stimuli we bring back into the analysis those emotional situations, those difficulties in living that are consequent upon unconscious problems.

The analysis itself in some aspect will be a constant stimulus for dreams. Sometimes it will be the actual material evoked; sometimes the analyst. As a rule it is easier to find this type of stimulus than the external one. I shall give one example of such an analytical stimulus to a dream. The patient's dream was " *There was a holy woman in whom the Cross was reflected.*" A dull and uneventful half-hour followed after the recital of this dream. The patient spoke of her wishes to become a " religious," and she spoke of visits to houses of retreat. Suddenly after a prolonged pause the patient said: " I've been looking at those french windows at the bottom of this room again. I did yesterday and I've been doing again what I did yesterday. It's so queer. The glass is all suffused with light, and the framework of wood down the centre and that cross piece near the top are so dark. But I close my eyes and what was light are then dark and the wood is all bright light and makes a cross. It's like having the cross in my eyes, so queer, because it's so big outside and yet the whole image is in my eyes." At this moment she removed her spectacles and I said: " Tell me what difference your spectacles make to your sight. Do you see more clearly with spectacles ? " To my great interest she said, " No, I see quite well without my spectacles. I wear them for my own comfort. Without them I feel so tall, so much larger, out of proportion, out of focus somehow with regard to other people. When I wear them I feel an ordinary size again."

The stimulus of the dream here in the analysis must have been an exact parallel to the days of infancy, the period of hallucinatory gratification. One does not often have demonstrated the physical basis of the psychical mechanism of introjection as clearly as this. " The holy woman in whom the Cross is reflected."

Sometimes a physical symptom will give the clue to a dream. The complaint of a feeling of hunger or emptiness will generally throw light on a dream. The patient to whom I have just referred started one analytical hour by reiterating the fact that she had a bad headache. It was manifestly very important that I should know she was suffering, how ill she felt. She finally exclaimed: " It's a murderous headache." She spent much time over this recital but eventually she remembered a dream. " Such a dream," she said, " I had last night. A murder had been committed and the murderer could not be found."

I desire therefore to focus your attention upon the question of stimuli for dreams, not as a thing to search for irrespective of all other problems of any hour, but as a factor to bear in mind. If found they will help in the elucidation of the dream, in the setting of the analytic work, and in the psychical problems of the moment with regard to the patient's life in the external world. If the stimuli of dreams are consistently omitted by the patient over a long period of time then the analyst needs to consider the problem of suppressed material and the patient's reasons for withholding it.

Here is another aspect of dreams. A long diffuse dream means that one need not look to the dream as being of any great help in the analytical hour unless there is some one particular element in it that is curious and likely to evoke associations.

The " Folkestone " dream was fairly long and yet not difficult to analyse. It yielded its meaning up through the hour. But that particular work was preliminary. There was no " grip " in the analysis of that day. The patient was quite amenable to my interpretation, since it was interesting to her intellectually. The analysis relieved no anxiety, raised none, threw no light on any problem of which she herself felt aware. Her problems had still to be reached.

Compare that long dream with the " lofty house " dream from the same patient quoted in this lecture. One can gauge of the progress of the analysis in that way. This patient will have long rambling dreams again, but I expect far fewer in the future. In the " lofty house " dream the analysis progressed. When analysis is progressing the dreams tend to be shorter, laconic, more baffling, more distorted. Of all dreams these are the most pregnant of meaning. They betray less in the manifest content. Occasionally after long resistance one may get an open dream expressing the very problem that has been resisted. As we get nearer strongholds of repression we must always expect to find problems exercising our patience. The dreams at the end of a lengthy analysis will be often the most difficult, the shortest and most recalcitrant of any, and one might add, the most worth while. In intervals of analysis during holidays and week-ends one finds dreams more prolific than during analytical periods. In a sequence of dreams of one night one can say that there is a disturbing affective content and a great effort to deal with this, and that the last dream of the series is likely to be less camouflaged than the others. Very often indeed, the last dream causes the patient to wake. I should direct attention during analysis to the last dream of such a series.

CHAPTER VII

ILLUSTRATIONS OF DREAMS OCCURRING DURING PSYCHICAL AND PHYSICAL CRISES

1. Dreams indicating the psychical condition of the patient at the beginning of analysis.
2. Dream foretelling a psychical breakdown.
3. " Fire " dreams and their import.
4. Dream foretelling a physical breakdown.
5. Dream showing psychical management of a crisis.

I PROPOSE to devote this chapter to the consideration of specific dreams related to me by patients during psychical crises of both lesser and greater moment. These dreams in their symbolical import are typical and so may be of value to the intending practitioner.

The " music " dream which was the first to be related in Chapter I was told to me by a patient during the early stage of analysis. She was suffering from the shock of an actual bereavement. The gratifications in the dream by night formed an extreme contrast to the desolation of her real life. This patient would fall asleep during the analytical sessions while she sucked the corner of a cushion. Subsequent analysis revealed a very profound conversion hysteria which had manifested itself at an early age.

My estimation of the " music " dream in view of the depth of the neurosis and further external traumas experienced during analysis is that it indicated in this patient some degree of promise that the psyche would withstand the stress it was called upon to bear from inner and outer causes. In the dream there is an hallucinatory return to the original sources of gratification which were also dramatized in the sucking of the cushion. It is a pleasure dream in which the instincts are directed in a normal manner to the objects of desire at the oral level. Periods of excessive anxiety, of deep depression, of suicidal phantasies, of physical illness were all experienced in due course by this patient. In estimating this dream of regression to oral gratification as holding the promise of renewed psychical health I take into account the fact that the patient never relinquished even at the times of greatest stress the routine duties of ordinary life and a degree of professional work.

At the beginning of the analysis, the falling asleep and the sucking of the cushion were themselves ways by which the patient began a healing process, being in fact comparable to the early suckling period. The non-interference of this on the part of the analyst, the allowing of the phase to run its course, meant the establishment of a deep trans-ference of a positive type. During this time too the suicidal tendencies had a mild and innocuous representation by her sleeping in my presence. Hence the advisability of non-interference with a safeguard against the development of more danger-ous forms of these tendencies.

A patient dreamt on several occasions within a period of a few weeks that *she was a very young child in a perambulator and that she was being wheeled along a beautiful sea front by her mother.*

This dream, like the " music " dream, is obvious in its uncamouflaged wish. There is no effort on the part of the different psychical mechanisms to distort the wish, there is no counter-wish being expressed. The psychical powers of resistance to a wish are at their minimum. With this patient the dream occurred in a critical period when the effort to continue ordinary life and work was only just maintained. The psychical crisis through which the patient was passing was the culmination of a period of analysis during which a fixed delusion passed away. By the crystallized delusion she had been able to maintain a degree of normality and thus remain at work, full of stress as this effort was. The weakening of the delusional belief necessitated an inner task of redistribution of psychical energy which hitherto had been dealt with by the cathexis in the delusion. In the delusion she projected on to a man various aggressive sexual acts. The delusion itself was in part the return of a repressed dissociated sexual trauma of childhood. The analytic work in connection with the early trauma made possible the release of the genuine Œdipus wishes with the accompanying hostility to the mother. Along with this release came memories of childhood deeds and phantasies that proved how strong had been not only aggressive phantasy but actual attempts to hurt the rival baby sister. The dream I have related represented a psychical respite for her feared aggressive impulses. By dreaming she was the only child she put herself in the position of one who had no need to be jealous and therefore no need to be afraid of aggressive impulses. She was, moreover, being looked after and safeguarded by her mother, and was therefore safe. One could look upon the dream as representing a wish for reconciliation with her mother. In estimating this dream as a favourable one from the point of prognosis I take the following data into consideration along with the import of the dream: The patient had retained contacts with the outer world by means of a fixed delusion; the delusion itself disappeared slowly while at the same time dynamic impulses of love and hate associated with the appropriate persons and correlated with specific and remembered situations of childhood came to light; the sublimations that became possible were not only reparative in import towards the mother but in themselves provided symbolical channels for fundamental instinct gratification. The dream, while representing a very strong desire to be a child again, can yet be regarded as a propitious one taking into account all the considerations which I have detailed.

The next dream is one that foretold a crisis. The woman who dreamt it was carrying on the arduous duties of a professional career at the time of the dream. These had made a great strain upon her actual physical strength in addition to the pyschical conflicts that were subsequently revealed. There was no conscious awareness of psychical illness at the time of the dream. She was experiencing lassitude and some lack of interest in her work. She assumed her interest would return in due course after a holiday which she felt she needed. The dream ran: "*I took up my watch to look at the time and found the face of the watch so covered over with strips of paper that I could not see what the time was.*"

Some time after this dream the woman, after a week's insomnia, was obliged to give up her professional duties and take a prolonged holiday during which she undertook a course of analysis that brought her psychoneurosis to light.

I cite this dream as one that heralded a physical and psychical breakdown. The dream recurred during the analytic treatment when the patient was on the way to recovery. The version of it then ran: "*I wanted to see what time it was and turned to look at my watch and it was not there. I then remembered I had put it on a shelf. I took it down and the face was quite clear so I could read the time.*"

I am here attempting no interpretation of the specific dream imagery. My purpose at the moment is to draw attention to the general import of a dream which was followed by a breakdown. Had this dream been related by the woman to a knowledgeable person she could have been advised to seek psychical help forthwith as definitely as one would advise a person with a rash to seek medical advice. Some amelioration of psychical stress would have prevented a complete breakdown.

Another " crisis " dream of general interest was told to me by a girl patient of fifteen who through the onset of psychical deafness was obliged to leave school. She was in a very unhappy state since the future held only gloomy prospects if she became deaf. *The dream in question represented a railway station in which all the trains had come to a standstill.* No trains came in, none went out. Engines had ceased to function. There was consequently no sound to be heard.

The analysis of this patient was a success. Her

psychical establishment has continued fifteen years and she is now a happily married woman. The dream regarded from the analyst's point of view was a helpful one for this reason: it gave one immediate clue concerning the purpose of the psychical deafness. Not to hear had the significance of magically causing engines to cease working. The whole subsequent analysis of this patient could be looked upon as the analysis of this dream. When by analytic technique the unconscious mind revealed the meanings associated with the engine symbol and the reasons for magically causing engines to stand still, the patient recovered her power of hearing.

I will now recount three dreams about fire related by three different patients.

The dreams are as follows:

(a) "*I saw a house on fire.* In it was a woman and her children. I saw a man go in to rescue them but he did not reappear, so he must have been burned as well."

(b) "*The house I was in was on fire.* I had great anxiety and prepared to escape but first I remembered my most precious possession, a picture I had been painting. It was not finished and I wanted to finish it. So I went to my studio and took it from the easel and then rushed from the burning house."

(c) "*I set my clothes on fire and woke up instantly.*"

These three dreams were each associated with a psychical crisis. The manifest content alone is worthy of consideration.

Each patient was passing through psychical stress caused by the aggressive impulses felt towards her mother. The reason for the aggressive attitude was the infantile jealousy aroused by the fact that the mother was given a child by the father. In the first dream we have quite simply stated the fact that mother and children are burned and finally the father himself who goes to the rescue is himself burned. Now this dream did not cause the patient concerned any distress in consciousness at all comparable with that experienced by the one who related the second dream. The mechanism of projection is partly the reason for this. It is illustrated in the dream by the fact that while the drama is enacted within the psyche, the " I," the ego, is an onlooker. The ego is not involved. In estimating how much stress the psyche can tolerate a dream of this kind is of use to the analyst. This patient is of the type who is more likely, if stress is too great, to be involved in accident or disaster caused externally than to cause it to herself personally. When she was a child, for example, this patient once rushed heedlessly into the street and was knocked down by a motor car.

The problem of dealing with aggressive impulses confronts also the second patient. The dream was associated with far more anxiety than that of the first patient. The " ego " is far more involved, for in the dream the patient is *within* the burning house. The projection mechanism is less strong than it is in the first dream. The house in the first dream symbolized the mother's body and children within it. The dreamer was distinct from it. In dream two, the house in which the dreamer found herself also symbolized the mother's body, but in contrast to the first dream, the dreamer was inside the body and danger to one endangered both. The libido, however, is stronger than the hate impulses. The wish to save is stronger than the desire to destroy. Hence one would conclude that this second patient will preserve psychical equilibrium in spite of distressing anxiety and the sublimation of both aggressive and libidinal impulses is given in the dream. The patient was a painter.

The third dream indicates a psychical crisis that may result in inflicting actual bodily harm. The projection mechanism is absent in the dream. Instead of " a house is on fire " we have " I set fire to myself." The ego is at the mercy of the aggressive wish. Such a dream as this may or may not be a precursor to an attempt at self-injury or in an extreme case to attempted suicide. But such a dream should cause the analyst to weigh up the situation.

The following are some of the considerations to be taken into account at such a time. The analyst must make some estimation of the strength of ego-development. The characteristic behaviour of the patient during emotional crises in the past will be an indication. Has the characteristic method of dealing with these been by flight, a breaking away from work and relationships ? Another criterion in analysis itself will be a change of mood from frankness to secrecy as if the patient were brooding over some plan. Another aspect of the patient's life which will help towards estimating eventualities is that of the general situation in reality. If interest in work is waning, if libidinal gratification direct and indirect is not being obtained, if human contacts are becoming fewer and attenuated or provoking only irritation, then one would take this dream as having a serious import. To summarize: If the patient who dreams in this way has not a well-integrated ego, if past emotional disturbances have been met by actual rupture of work and friendships, by sudden flight, and if at the time of the dream the whole situation in reality presents the picture of frustrated libidinal satisfaction and uncanalized inarticulate aggression then if the patient becomes brooding and inaccessible one could rightly surmise that some attempt at self-destruction was probable. Temporary measures to deal with the crisis must then be adopted and pursued until it is passed.

The following dream is interesting because it was the prelude to a physical illness. The person who dreamt it had been carrying on strenuous work in spite of excessive lassitude for which she hesitated to consult a doctor since she had no actual physical symptoms. *She dreamt that she was clinging with all her might to a window ledge and then finally exhausted she fell to the ground.* Two days after this dream the woman fell to the ground in a fainting condition, the first experience of fainting she had known. A doctor was called in and he found that she must have been suffering from an infection of the bladder for some time. There was an illness of three months' duration before the patient recovered.

I will give one further dream indicating the psychical management of a minor crisis. In this case the patient had had a considerable experience of analytic treatment. During this period psychical stress concerning aggression had most often been symbolized in her dreams by fierce angry seas. These usually were in pursuit of her, threatening to drown and overwhelm her. On the occasion of the dream to which I refer, when a father-surrogate figure had died, *she dreamt that she was in deep water. The water however was so briny that it held her up and she knew that there was no fear of drowning.* The association to " salt water " was immediately " salt tears " and then the next moment the patient quoted the lines:

Let Love clasp Grief, lest both be drowned.

There is no menace to the ego in this psychical situation. Another patient of mine successfully working through this kind of crisis in connection with a personal loss, wrote:

Leave me my grief. Thus, undisturbed
By clamorous help, I still may weep.
While tears can flow
Love is not dead.

CHAPTER VIII

PSYCHICAL READJUSTMENTS INDICATED IN DREAMS

1. Dreams illustrating the progress being made in the analysis.
2. Deductions concerning psychical changes from the manifest content of dreams related over a period of analysis.
3. Dreams indicating sexual development.
4. Dreams indicating modifications of the super-ego.
5. Characteristics of a dream analysis indicating the patient's ability to deal effectively with his psychical problems.

DURING the course of an analysis that lasts over a considerable period psychical changes and re-adjustments taking place are from time to time to be perceived in the patient's dreams. Indeed, one criterion the analyst can use in estimating a patient's ability to deal with his own psychical stress will be found in the nature of his dreams. I propose to illustrate by dream material the way in which these changes are manifested.

Here are three dreams told to me by three patients during the course of their analysis. The first one was related to me in the following way: " *I was in an underground station and undecided about boarding a train. I got in though and after a while the train stopped at a station called ' Bentley.' I got out and saw the station was not underground but above board—I mean above ground.*"

This dream indicated a fresh adjustment in the patient's psyche and a definite stage in the analysis.

The station " Bentley " brought to the patient's mind the fact that he had as a child called his elder brother " Bentley " at a time when he himself could not pronounce the word " beastly." This dream heralded the recovery from repression of emotional attitudes and specific behaviour towards the elder brother. The " station " was no longer underground but " above board."

The second dream was related by a young woman patient. It ran: *I was sitting on a sofa and Douglas Fairbanks was making love to me. After a time he became my brother and I grew anxious and gradually woke up, but it was as if voices around me were saying " poor kid."*

In the analysis of this dream it was clear that Douglas Fairbanks referred to both father and son. Hence when the film actor became the dreamer's brother, her father also was in her dream thoughts and wishes. The " love-making " on the sofa had specific reference to the transference situation in the analysis. In the same way the " voices " in the room in the dream saying " poor kid " referred to the analyst as " voice."

This dream indicated the progress of psychical adjustment and a definite stage in the analysis. The unconscious Œdipus wishes and the transference of these upon the analyst have become articulate in the dream. The modification of the super-ego is apparent in the sympathetic " voices."

The third dream is taken from the analysis of a patient who had suffered from profound conversion hysteria. In relating the dream the patient said *" the dream has a theatrical air about it as if it were an ' acting ' and the people in it were puppets. There was scenery and a signpost indicating a desolate road. The signpost had on it the name of a battlefield in the last war, and so that meant doing it all over again. There was the figure of a man in white, like a cook.*"

This dream definitely indicated the struggle in the patient's psyche between " doing it all over again," i.e. another repetition of conversion symptoms or a return to healthy life. The conversion symptoms were represented by the ideas of " theatrical," " acting," " cooking," " doing it all over again." The patient herself realized this and hence this dream is indicative of psychical readjustment. The situation became clear during the analytical hour in the following narration. The patient remarked, " I rang up my friend yesterday and I asked her how she liked her new job. She said she hadn't started because she became sick. I said 'Bad luck, but you will be all right, it won't happen again; you will be successful next time.' She said, ' I suppose so,' but she said it reluctantly as if she were loath to be successful, loath to give up being ill." After this narration the patient realized the cogency of her remarks about her friend in reference to herself and in the light of the dream. The patient is becoming self-enlightened, and the resolution of conflicts producing bodily symptoms is within sight.

Here is another method of judging psychical changes being made during the course of analytic treatment. From one patient's analysis I select three dreams related to me at lengthy intervals.

The first was this: " *I was in a room with my wife at the bottom of the ocean.*" This dream occurred at the beginning of the analysis. I am not here concerned with the significance of the symbolism, nor

DA—L

the actual associations the patient supplied which made an interpretation possible in the hour the dream was related.

I want to compare this dream in the manifest content with a second which followed some months later. The second dream was: "*I saw a great lizard which at first I thought was part of the bark of a tree slowly uncurl itself and separate from the tree. I saw a groove in the tree trunk into which it exactly fitted. After disengaging itself from the tree as if to get free altogether, it changed its mind and curled back and became one with the tree again.*"

This dream during the analytical hour yielded by the patient's associations some of the meaning of the *latent* content, and therefore the significance of the symbolism. The analyst however can draw deductions from the change in manifest content between the first and second dream concerning the psychical work done by the analysis during the interval. The neurosis from which the patient suffered was of the type generally called narcissistic. The first dream represents the narcissistic state very well in the picture given of profound isolation and insulation. The second dream is staged above ground in a habitable world, although the dreamer represents a part of himself as a huge parasite afraid of separation. The patient woke from this dream in anxiety, a sign in itself of the weakening of narcissistic defences.

The third dream, which followed after a considerable interval, was: "*I was in an hotel lounge when there was an alarm that the house across the way was on fire. Others went to the rescue. I started to go with them but when I reached the door I turned back to the lounge.*"

Again this dream yielded specific associations during the hour when it was related and interpretations were given in terms of those associations. But the analyst can measure the slow psychical changes being effected by the analytic work in contrasting the manifest content of this dream with the last one. The patient represents himself no longer as a lizard. He is a man, albeit an inmate of a lounge (lounge-lizard). Again he makes an attempt to leave the comfort of his lounge and then turns back. Yet since his mind stages the dream, the men who go to the rescue are aspects of himself too. One can hope that in due time continued analysis will bring him to the stage where he is able to face and deal with his own aggressive impulses (indicated by the burning house) against which the narcissistic defences were organized.

The comments on these three dreams I have given are not to be taken as the *analysis* of them. I have not given the analytic work done on them, nor were these comments made to the patient. I have selected the dreams for the purpose of showing that by such contrasts and comparisons of the manifest content of dreams the analyst can make a surmise of the psychical changes that the actual analytic work is effecting.

I will give next a series of dreams occurring at intervals over the course of a lengthy analysis. Again, I am not here concerned with the actual interpretations of the material supplied by the patient on the several occasions of the dreams. I wish simply to direct attention to the changes in the manifest content indicative of changing orientations during the analysis.

The first version of the theme was a nightmare which occurred several times in the same form. It ran: "*I found a piece of cotton in my mouth and began to pull it out. After pulling a long time I dare pull no longer for I felt it was attached to some inner organ which might come out with it. I woke in terror.*"

The next variant of the dream was that hair was substituted for cotton. The next variant was that instead of cotton or hair the substance pulled out was thick and almost choked the dreamer. The fourth variant after two years' analysis was: "*I said to you I only understand the process of introjection by thinking of the muscles which run into and form the eyeball itself.*"

The last and final version of the theme was a *dream in which the patient was again taking a hair out of her mouth. It came out quite easily, it was not attached to anything, and no anxiety was felt in the dream.*

These dreams contain the clues to the major problems of the patient's neurosis. The whole analysis could be looked upon as an elucidation of their latent content. The element of "cotton," "thread," "hair," for example, had not only immense unconscious symbolic significance, but at the same time was the one that bridged the unconscious phantasy with real experiences from earliest infancy to late childhood. External situations arousing anxiety were linked with this all-dominating theme of thread. I made a reference to this almost exclusive use of one symbol in Chapter II and these dreams were related by the patient to whom I there referred.

For the analyst the changes in the manifest content of these dreams is an evidence of the changing psychical struggle, while the culminating dream is an indication that the problem had reached solution and the anxiety caused by it had been resolved.

I would draw your attention again to the water dreams to which I referred in the previous chapter. In addition to the specific interpretation pertinent to the patient's associations in relation to a single dream in which anxiety is experienced concerning water, the analyst can also judge in recurring dreams of this kind of the progress made in the resolution of anxiety. For example, if a patient who at times of stress has dreamt of terrifying seas responds after a period of analysis to psychical painful stimuli by dreaming of floating on water and a certainty of not drowning, the analyst may well conclude that sufficient readjustment has been made to enable the patient to deal with his own inner problems.

Another type of criterion may be used in relation to dreams to estimate the progress of internal psychical adjustments. I have found that patients suffering from disorders of the melancholic type and profound conversion hysteria will have dreams over a long period of time that concern themselves with either parts of objects which are symbolical of parts of the body or with these same parts of the body directly without symbolism. For example, in the case of one such type of patient, fragments of dreams remembered have been such visual images as a crevice in a wall, flagstones with grass between the flags, part of a tree showing three excrescences, a bracket on a wall, a part of a woman with genitals exposed, a man's exposed penis, the curve of the breasts, the larger curves of the buttocks, circular discs that symbolized the anus, vertical lines close together symbolizing the vagina, and horizontal lines symbolizing the mouth.

When dreams of this type are continuous over a long period of time the patient is dealing with part-object relationships that belong to the oral and anal-sadistic phase of development, and conflicts crystallized at this time which have never been resolved.

If the analysis can deal with the infantile problem as re-staged in the transference situation, the nature of the dreams will change. Instead of dreams the sole content of which is part of a whole we shall have instead whole persons whose " parts " are important. In addition to this we shall find situations dramatized between " whole " people and these will not be exclusively based on the major conflict of the neurosis, namely the fear of aggressive impulses, the fear of the object's aggression and the varying defences against both. For example, after a long series of dreams of the type I have been indicating, the patient who dreamt of a tree showing three excrescences dreamt the next night that she was giving flowers to a woman who had been ill. The significances of the three excrescences were very over-determined and their many different meanings do not concern me here. One meaning alone is pertinent, namely that they symbolized three children of her mother's who had died. The conjunction of that dream with the one in which the dreamer was giving living flowers to a woman who had been ill, the meaning of which is clear, illustrates the fact that psychical development is taking place, that loving impulses are less throttled by the aggressive ones.

Again, where the nature of the psychical disturbance is not as profound as indicated by the type of dreams I have just illustrated, the general trend of dreams will indicate to the analyst the kind of psychical movement that is taking place through the analysis. For example, dreams which hold within them the clues to anal phantasies, and situations in childhood involving both the child's behaviour and the behaviour of the environment to the child, may continue for a long time. At last, however, the nature of the dreams will change and oral or genital interests will become predominant. Correspondingly the predominant figure in dreams for a long time may be analyst-mother, at another time analyst-father, or sister and brother with the appropriate emotional attitudes.

A succession of homo-sexual dreams will give place at last to the emergence of hetero-sexual ones. This is indicative of the progress in analysis. At the same time, we may see in dreams the ebb and flow of tentative adjustments going on in the psyche long before stabilization is reached. A seeming retrogression and submergence into old attitudes will occur but adjustments will again reassert themselves with more strength.

Dreams that indicate the modification of the severity of the infantile super-ego are a welcome evidence of the development of the psyche. Here are three examples of this.

1. " *I was driving in my car and something happened, I don't know what, but I nearly had an accident. It was my fault I know and I saw the policeman and*

was quite agitated. To my surprise he seemed quite friendly."

2. "*A child was being naughty. Someone was very angry with it and I felt angry too but instead of scolding I went to the child and comforted it.*"

3. "*A child had made water on the floor and it was terrified. I went to it and helped it to mop up the water.*"

Each of these dreams evoked specific associations belonging to present-day anxieties as well as historical situations and these were the concern of the analytical hour. In addition to these, however, the analyst could deduce that adjustments towards psychical ease were being made, accommodations and tolerance within the psyche being effected.

I will give another aspect of dreams that indicates readjustments within the psyche. A patient suffering from a deep-seated conversion hysteria called upon to face specific external stimuli became bodily ill and was obliged to go to bed, with doctor and nurse in attendance. Eighteen months later, after continuous analysis, external stimuli of the same nature as in the first instance were again encountered. Excessive anxiety was experienced but the patient maintained to a greater degree the regular routine of life. She dreamt that "*Mr. X was in a nursing home.*" The dream here indicates the psychical progress. First of all she *dreams* of illness instead of being actually bodily ill herself. Secondly, she has projected the illness on to Mr. X, a father-surrogate. In other words in the conflict concerning her frustrated libidinal wishes and the ensuing hostility to the thwarting father and fear of him she is no longer incorporating the injured and dying man and *being* him in herself, thus punishing herself, but we have a separation of herself from him. He is at last externalized. If this patient can continue to bear the anxiety concerning her hostile wishes due to frustration, and analysis can modify and resolve this, then the return to actual bodily symptoms will no longer be necessary.

A delusional patient of mine had a recurrent dream in which a girl of her own age was crying bitterly. The dreamer saw herself try to comfort the girl and to elicit from her what was the cause of her trouble, but she always failed. The dream occurred several times during the first three years of analysis. The fixed delusion disappeared as well as the static picture she represented to me of her childhood together with the static range of her emotions and external interests. When the analysis began to reach the truth of both her environment in childhood and her own emotional life lived in that environment there was no recurrence of the dream I have related. The non-recurrence of a specific dream may therefore indicate to the analyst that a repressed psychical conflict has been resolved.

Again, with patients who have been subject to alcoholic excess I have found that when they *dream* of drunkenness instead of actually becoming drunk, one has reached a stage where the psychical causes of the habit are becoming accessible and therefore hopeful of solution. The same thing applies when a fetishist dreams of his fetish, and a person subject to actual compulsive masturbation during waking hours dreams of it in sleep.

Finally, I will give some account of a dream which I consider gives a good indication that the patient's analysis is reaching the stage when the end of analytic work can be considered.

The dream ran: " *I had climbed to the top of a place and then I had to come down, but at first it seemed impossible. Still I'd climbed up and if I could do that I surely could get back. So I started, at first the distance below was terrifying but at last I came to the last bit where there was no further foothold, so I had to jump that and it was not difficult, I did it easily.*"

The person who dreamt this had had a lengthy analysis, and from this dream I concluded that he had reached a stage when the prospect of definitely terminating the analysis could be brought forward.

The external stimuli at the time of the dream was the fact that the patient had forgone a full-time paid appointment for a half-time one in order that he might begin to build up a private practice. He had no private means so that he faced a risk in doing this as he had domestic obligations. That he had done this was in itself a proof of growing inner confidence.

The actual analysis itself for some time prior to this dream had brought elucidation of anal phantasies and anal defences against castration fears. Direct rivalry and hostility to the father on the genital level had been elaborated in the transference. The effect of this in reality was a giving-up of some routine work and the facing of a situation of rivalry with others with whom he would compete in building up a private practice. Doubts concerning potency came to light and with them the unconscious fears of the woman's genital based on the phantasies of its being a dangerous place because of its being a wound caused by an attack.

The day before the dream the patient said in the course of the analytical work, " Dr. X says it is dangerous to do analytic work with a woman when in a state of depression." I was able before the hour was over, by means of the patient's associations, to bring to light the fact that this remark covered first of all his anxiety concerning the practice of psychoanalysis on which he was about to embark, and secondly that this fear was unconsciously concerned with the phantasies of the vagina. When he said, for example, " if you work in the depression you may make the woman worse," he was unconsciously expressing his fear concerning sexual intercourse because of phantasies of the vagina as a wounded place. The next day the patient told me the dream I have already related. The associations during the course of the hour were analytically of great importance. They yielded historical material that provided definite data concerning the places where during his first three years he would have had opportunity of seeing the female genitals. Experience of early erections was deducible from the material along with evidence of early masturbation. The house up which he climbed in the dream was symbolically the female body and references to his mother and sisters in his babyhood and childhood days were many. During his meditation on the dream during the hour he said, " I had climbed up and then had to come down, but I expect the problem is how to get up again. I mean, we come down and out at birth from the mother, but we never get back wholly to the womb again.

It is a part of the body only that returns in adult intercourse."

Before the end of the hour the patient said, " And I know my analysis must stop. I'm nearly at the end of my training and if I get patients that will mean another step towards the end."

This dream is a masturbation phantasy; it is a reassurance dream but the assurance is well founded. Analytically considered, the associations showed great plasticity, ranged from the present day to earliest infantile experiences, and were integrally linked together. The same confidence was expressed in thoughts concerning birth, anal functioning and genital power. When this consistency of mood and attitude manifests itself in relation to experiences that range from infancy to the present day indicated by a dream, when the patient is planning his future hopefully and taking risks on it to achieve his aims, the analyst can with confidence think the analysis is within sight of a propitious close. Especially is this so when the patient himself foreshadows it, and feels the separation from the analyst (here representing both parental figures) to be almost due and is evidently preparing for it.

There is another aspect of dream-analysis from which the analyst can estimate that successful re-adjustments are being made. The patient will gain perspective with regard to his past life. Associations to dreams will cease to be exclusively an expression of stereotyped attitudes and the repetition of static memories. If the archaic super-ego becomes dis-integrated so also does the devil himself. Parents are more truly seen as human beings as the patient becomes human. This change of tone in recalling memory pictures is a fascinating one. It is as if the freed libido travelled back as well as forward. Suddenly one hears, " How patient Nannie was with me. I can see that now," or as if never realized before, " That was a lovely garden we had. I am glad I had my childhood there." In the same way a patient will be able to face with more equanimity and tolerance the real injustices and hardships dealt out to him in childhood. Past loves and joys as well as repressed hates are rescued from oblivion and enrich the psyche. This to my mind is one criterion of a successful analysis. The libido, the true phœnix, emerges again. In that renewal are two factors; anxiety concerning aggression and phantastic fears for bodily safety are mitigated and reduced, and, secondly, the past libidinal strivings are rescued from oblivion and merged into a more unified positive attitude to life.

CHAPTER IX

" ANALYSED " PERSONS AND THEIR DREAMS

1. Dreams fulfil the same functions for " analysed " and " unanalysed " persons.
2. Dreams related by " analysed " persons and the changes in affective attitude with regard to them achieved by analysis.
3. Dreams of " normal " unanalysed persons.
4. " Analysis " and " Synthesis."

THE type of " analysed " person to whom I refer in this chapter is one who has had an analysis adequate enough to ensure not only ego-stability, that is the capacity to carry on an independent life effectively, but also one in which direct instinct gratification and sublimation is accompanied by zest and a feeling of well-being. I refer to the dreams of people who have achieved this result through analytic work and I do not include those whose analysis has not been carried through to this achievement.

The " analysed " person like the " unanalysed " will continue to dream. Analysis does not analyse away the " unconscious." Instinctual drives remain. The fundamental infantile " wishes " themselves are as timeless as the inherited instinctual life. The dreams of the " analysed " no less than the " un-analysed " are psychical attempts to deal with inner and outer stimuli leading to excitation of anxiety. The dream does the same service for the " analysed "

as the "unanalysed." Its function is to preserve
sleep by the conversion of disturbances into fulfilled
infantile wishes the disguise of which is achieved by
the various dream mechanisms. From that point
of view there is no difference whatever between the
dreams of the "unanalysed" and the "analysed."
The unconscious wishes are the same, the same
mechanisms to distort these wishes are used in such
a way as to accommodate the demands both of the
id and the super-ego. The difference then lies
neither in the dream mechanisms nor in the fundamental unconscious wishes.

I will proceed to examine the nature of the
difference and I will give a specific example as an
illustration. When a person is being analysed actual
childhood incidents concerned with anal functioning and anal phantasies are accompanied by affects
such as shame and anger. Dreams related to these
phantasies and memories will be greatly disguised
and much analytical work will be done before
highly-charged affects will lose their intensity and
the reasons for these affects understood.

An "analysed" person talking to me concerning
the nature of the differences between dreams before
and after analysis said, "Before analysis, or during
the early stages of analysis, a dream I had last week
would have produced the most painful and disturbing affect though presented in a disguised way.
I dreamt *I was a little child sitting on a lavatory seat
and producing a vast amount of excreta.* The contrast
was that in the first place the dream was undisguised and secondly the affect was different. When
I remembered the dream in the morning I smiled
inwardly to myself at that industrious child. Later

193

I did a good day's work with a pleasant knowledge of real accomplishment."

Another " analysed " person told me a dream which she said would have produced an unpleasant feeling-tone throughout the next day if she had had one of the same import before or during analysis. The *dream was that she was a small child pirouetting round a room to display a grand frock.* The comment on this was: " I recognized the previous day's stimulus for the dream and during the day it did not recur to me again. I had a pleasurably-toned day, not exaggerated in any way. In the evening when I went to bed I thought that I had been quite entertaining and amusing to the company who had been present at dinner. Then I remembered my dream."

Here is a third dream of an " analysed " person. " *I dreamt that Mr. and Mrs. X were being divorced, and that it could only have as its sequel that I should marry Mr. X.*" The comment on this dream was: " The stimulus for that dream was that married friends of mine, Mr. and Mrs. A, sent me some flowers. Mr. X in the dream is a man older than myself. He was an important figure in my childhood and quite clearly a father-surrogate. The infantile father-transference was stimulated by the gift of flowers so that the wish to separate Mr. and Mrs. X, the parental figures in the dream, and so to marry Mr. X is in the present day brought up to date in the unconscious phantasy of separating Mr. A from his wife and bearing his child." I asked: " What affect did the dream produce ? " The reply given was: " No disturbing affect at all. I recognized the stimulus, the meaning of the dream, and said,

"Here we are again, same old story in its latest setting. It didn't shock me or agitate me. Mr. A is an attractive man. Oh! by the way, I've finished that article for the —— *Journal*. I think it's good and I feel pretty sure the Editor will accept it." These three dreams with the context and accompanying real life of the dreamer illustrate very well some characteristics of dreams of " analysed " persons. The significance of the primitive impulses is accepted. There is no repudiation. What has been analysed, and therefore modified, is the severity of the super-ego the effect of which is to inhibit or stultify not only direct gratification but also sub-limatory processes. A greater integrity between the body-ego and psychical ego has been achieved and the phases of development are knit together. For example, the tiny child who performs its excretory functions with loving pride is in its unconscious phantasies making a wonderful gift to its parent, and on such a fundamental pattern is based the power of the adult to achieve results from activities undertaken willingly.

A patient suffering from psychical deafness to whom I have referred in Chapter VII brought to me during analysis a number of dreams in which the repressed desire to be the centre of attraction was expressed in many ways. She was in reality at the time very shy and self-conscious. On days when she had these dreams she found it impossible to go into a public dining-room and would if she could take her meals alone. During analysis the need for excessive exhibitionism was itself modified because the causes were understood, but the result of this was that the natural impulse found a satisfactory channel and in later years she was at home on a lecture platform and found no difficulty in dealing with large classes of adult students.

In the " exhibition " dream of the " analysed " person I have given, the primitive impulse was recognized, accepted, and the affect was pleasant, while the sublimation into lively and interesting talk in company took place *un*consciously.

After the " Œdipus " dream, the " analysed " person experienced no disturbing conflict such as would occur in some way if the person were an-analysed, especially if that person had no satis-factory love-life or sublimatory work. In the given instance it is clear to see that although the un-conscious infantile wishes are indestructible, the infantile demand for fulfilment of those wishes in reality, that is, actually to separate two people who represent the parents, has not only become less imperative, it has been relinquished. The infantile wish to bear a child to the *father* has become sublimated. After relating the dream the speaker immediately in her reference to the finished article and the prospect of the editor accepting it made quite clear how canalization of energy had led to a symbolic fulfilment of infantile wishes, one compatible with the ego-ideal and in terms of reality.

My comments on these dreams brings me immediately both to general characteristics of the dreams of the " analysed " as contrasted with those of the " unanalysed " and the reasons for them.

" Analysed " persons who dreamt prolifically before analysis subsequently find their dreams greatly reduced in number. People who dreamt either not at all (that is, did not remember) or only rarely remembered dreams, find their dreams more accessible during and after analysis. Prolific dreaming indicates a great deal of unresolved internal conflict. The dreams are attempts to deal with this. Conversely, entire absence of dreams indicates some faulty working in the psychic apparatus. The " analysed " person finds in his dreams a key to the anxiety and emotional disturbance he will inevitably experience in life, since by these dreams he will be able to correlate external disturbing events with unconscious impulses, desires, phantasies and so to a great degree control and manage appropriately the associated affects. The " analysed " person will experience only rarely if at all " anxiety " dreams. Nightmares seldom occur, neither do dreams in which animals represent the animal nature of the dreamer.

The " analysed " person will not experience the repetitive dream nor will there occur long series of dreams representing parts of things as parts of bodies. The dreams tend on the whole to be much shorter than before analysis; the long complicated dream is rare just as is the very beautiful type of dream. The main reason for this is the fact that analysis has made possible greater satisfaction in reality, as regards both direct instinct gratification and sublimation. Hence a person whose achievements have been mainly in dreams and not executed in reality may well lose his pleasurable night dreams but find his inhibitions in doing actual work in reality removed.

I have indicated the main differences in dreams experienced by persons before and after a course of psycho-analysis. The dreams of "unanalysed" people approximate to those of "normal" people.

The rough standard of normality I have in mind is the ability to lead an ordinary life in which love, work and recreation have their place. But this rough standard includes varying degrees of psychical stability. The most stabilized people when threatened by external disaster experience psychical stress which may manifest itself in disturbing dreams. Normal people who are not so psychically well-stabilized more often have nightmares or recurrent anxiety dreams. These produce a disagreeable affect during waking hours. Such dreams are often attributed to the meal of the evening before while the disagreeable affect felt during the day is attributed (that is, rationalized) to some minor happening in actuality. The "sulks," "bad temper," "impatience," the "fit of the blues," of normal people have the same origin as the neuroses of those who recognize themselves as psychologically ill.

The dreams of "normal" people are very seldom as undisguised as those I have quoted from "analysed" persons. The laws of dream formation produce a manifest dream content that successfully disguises the true sources of the conflict producing it.

The analysis of dreams involves a disintegration of the manifest content in order to reach the emotions and memories that the ego has repudiated. The condensations are elaborated, affect is set free by discovery of the element from which it has been displaced, symbolism is uncovered, repressed memories and phantasies are brought to light. But while this technique is termed " analysis " and the therapy associated with it is called " psycho-analysis " we must not neglect the fact that it is precisely the " analysis " that sets in motion a corresponding synthesis. The two are inseparable. The mechanisms within the mind which mould the unconscious psychical material into a presentable form are innate psychological processes. These are in no way disturbed by expert analysis. Analysis of dream content, liberation of affect, and conscious understanding render possible the operation of these innate processes over wider tracks of the psychic life to the advantage of the psychical ego in reality. Only by effective displacement and sym-bolization on to the external world is sublimation possible. The breaking up of dreams in the pro-cess of psycho-analytic technique is one of the processes that enables the inner psychological forces to bring about a new synthesis. In calling the technique psycho-analysis we lay stress upon the technician's art. Tacitly, however, we acknowledge that the new synthesis is brought about by the forces within the psyche itself. The recuperative powers lie within. The technician by analysis removes whatever stultifies them.

CHAPTER X

A "LAST" DREAM

I WISH to record as the final dream in this book one which was in reality a last dream, since it was related by a woman three days before her death. She did not regain full consciousness after reciting it. Physical distress had mainly been caused by persistent sickness and her dream ran: " *I saw all my sicknesses gathered together and as I looked they were no longer sicknesses but roses and I knew the roses would be planted and that they would grow.*"

I wish to make only a short comment on this "last" dream, since the psycho-analyst will have no difficulty in finding significances from the manifest content according to his general and particular insight.

Let me rather close this book not by interpretation but by a reference to the foundations of our belief in the practice of psycho-analysis.

The woman whose dream I have related was eighty-one years of age. She had suffered many vicissitudes in her long life, any one of which would have brought despair to a less stabilized character. Her mental faculties suffered no diminution. She shared in her old age the interests of youth and any movement that promised fairer and better conditions for mankind in the future appealed alike to her mind and heart, and among these was psycho-analysis. The dream reveals the source of the un-failing hope which sustained the dreamer in life and was her consolation in death.

It is Eros alone who *knows* that the roses will be planted and will grow.

APPENDIX

APPENDIX

APPENDIX

BIBLIOGRAPHY

FREUD, SIGMUND, *The Interpretation of Dreams*. Translated by James Strachey in the *Standard Edition of the Complete Psychological Works of Sigmund Freud*, Vols IV and V (London: The Hogarth Press, 1953; New York: W. W. Norton).

GRODDECK, GEORG, *The Meaning of Illness* (London: The Hogarth Press, 1977; New York; International Universities Press).

JONES, ERNEST, *Papers on Psycho-Analysis* (London: Bailliere, 1948; Boston: Beacon Press 1961).

KLEIN, MELANIE, *The Psycho-Analysis of Children* (London: The Hogarth Press, 1975; Boston: Seymour Lawrence, 1976).

LACAN, JACQUES, *The Four Fundamental Concepts of Psycho-Analysis* (London: The Hogarth Press, 1977; New York: W. W. Norton, 1978).

LOWES, J. LIVINGSTON, *The Road to Xanadu* (London: Constable, 1927).

PRESCOTT, "Poetry and Dreams." *Journal of Abnormal Psychology*, Vol. VII, Nos. 1 and 2. April-June 1912.

QUILLER-COUCH, SIR ARTHUR, *On the Art of Writing. The Difference between Prose and Verse* (London: Cambridge University Press, 1916).

RANK, O., and SACHS, H., *Die Bedeutung der Psychoanalyse für die Geisteswissenschaften*, No. 93, Wiesbaden. (*Trans.: The Significance of Psychoanalysis for the Mental Sciences*, New York, 1916).

WEEKLEY, ERNEST, *Romance of Words* (London: Murray, 1912).

WILLIS, GEORGE, *Philosophy of Speech* (London: Allen & Unwin, 1920).

INDEX

207

INDEX